D1301317

# Image and Video Encryption
## From Digital Rights Management to Secured Personal Communication

# Advances in Information Security

## Sushil Jajodia
*Consulting editor*
*Center for Secure Information Systems*
*George Mason University*
*Fairfax, VA 22030-4444*
*email: jajodia@gmu.edu*

The goals of Kluwer International Series on ADVANCES IN INFORMATION SECURITY are, one, to establish the state of the art of, and set the course for future research in information security and, two, to serve as a central reference source for advanced and timely topics in information security research and development. The scope of this series includes all aspects of computer and network security and related areas such as fault tolerance and software assurance.

ADVANCES IN INFORMATION SECURITY aims to publish thorough and cohesive overviews of specific topics in information security, as well as works that are larger in scope or that contain more detailed background information than can be accommodated in shorter survey articles. The series also serves as a forum for topics that may not have reached a level of maturity to warrant a comprehensive textbook treatment.

Researchers as well as developers are encouraged to contact Professor Sushil Jajodia with ideas for books under this series.

### *Additional titles in the series:*

*INTRUSION DETECTION AND CORRELATION: Challenges and Solutions* by Christopher Kruegel, Fredrik Valeur and Giovanni Vigna; ISBN: 0-387-23398-9

*THE AUSTIN PROTOCOL COMPILER* by Tommy M. McGuire and Mohamed G. Gouda; ISBN: 0-387-23227-3

*ECONOMICS OF INFORMATION SECURITY* by L. Jean Camp and Stephen Lewis; ISBN: 1-4020-8089-1

*PRIMALITY TESTING AND INTEGER FACTORIZATION IN PUBLIC KEY CRYPTOGRAPHY* by Song Y. Yan; ISBN: 1-4020-7649-5

*SYNCHRONIZING E-SECURITY* by Godfried B. Williams; ISBN: 1-4020-7646-0

*INTRUSION DETECTION IN DISTRIBUTED SYSTEMS:*
*An Abstraction-Based Approach* by Peng Ning, Sushil Jajodia and X. Sean Wang ISBN: 1-4020-7624-X

*SECURE ELECTRONIC VOTING* edited by Dimitris A. Gritzalis; ISBN: 1-4020-7301-1

*DISSEMINATING SECURITY UPDATES AT INTERNET SCALE* by Jun Li, Peter Reiher, Gerald J. Popek; ISBN: 1-4020-7305-4

*SECURE ELECTRONIC VOTING* by Dimitris A. Gritzalis; ISBN: 1-4020-7301-1

*APPLICATIONS OF DATA MINING IN COMPUTER SECURITY*, edited by Daniel Barbará, Sushil Jajodia; ISBN: 1-4020-7054-3

*MOBILE COMPUTATION WITH FUNCTIONS* by Zeliha Dilsun Kırlı, ISBN: 1-4020-7024-1

*Additional information about this series can be obtained from*
http://www.wkap.nl/prod/s/ADIS

# Image and Video Encryption
## From Digital Rights Management to
## Secured Personal Communication

by

**Andreas Uhl**
**Andreas Pommer**
*Salzburg University, Austria*

 Springer

Library of Congress Cataloging-in-Publication Data

A C.I.P. Catalogue record for this book is available
from the Library of Congress.

IMAGE AND VIDEO ENCRYPTION
From Digital Rights Management to Secured Personal Communication
by Andreas Uhl and Andreas Pommer
Dept. of Scientific Computing, Salzburg University, Austria

Advances in Information Security  Volume 15

ISBN 0-387-23402-0          e-ISBN 0-387-23403-9

Printed on acid-free paper.

Printed in the United States of America.

9 8 7 6 5 4 3 2 1          SPIN 11053811, 11332510

springeronline.com

*I dedicate this book to my wife Jutta – thank you for your understanding and help in my ambition to be both, a loving and committed partner and father as well as an enthusiastic scientist.*

*Andreas Uhl*

*I dedicate this book to all the people with great ideas who make the net an enjoyable place.*

*Andreas Pommer*

# Contents

Dedication     v

List of Figures     ix

List of Tables     xiii

Preface     xv

Acknowledgments     xvii

1. INTRODUCTION     1

2. VISUAL DATA FORMATS     11
   1. Image and Video Data     11
   2. DCT-based Systems     12
   3. Wavelet-based Systems     14
   4. Further Techniques     18

3. CRYPTOGRAPHY PRIMER     21
   1. Introduction, Terminology     21
   2. Secret key vs. Public key Cryptography     22
   3. Block Ciphers     23
   4. Stream Ciphers     27
   5. Hybrid Algorithms, some Applications     28
   6. Cryptanalysis Overview     29
   7. Further Information     30

4. APPLICATION SCENARIOS FOR THE ENCRYPTION OF VISUAL DATA     31
   1. Security provided by Infrastructure or Application     31
   2. Full Encryption vs. Selective Encryption     32
   3. Interplay between Compression and Encryption     37

5.  IMAGE AND VIDEO ENCRYPTION                                    45
    1    DCT-based Techniques                                     47
    2    Wavelet-based Techniques                                 82
    3    Further Techniques                                      115
    4    Transparent Encryption                                  127
    5    Commercial Applications and Standards                   129

6.  CONCLUSIONS                                                  135

Appendices                                                       137
A   Copyrighted sections                                         137
B   Test Images and Videos                                       139
    1    Cover Page                                              139
    2    Test Images                                             139
    3    Sequence 1 — Bowing                                     141
    4    Sequence 2 — Surf Side                                  141
    5    Sequence 3 — Coast Guard                                141
    6    Sequence 4 — Akiyo                                      142
    7    Sequence 5 — Calendar                                   142
C   Authors' Biographies                                         143

References                                                       145

Index                                                            159

# List of Figures

2.1   Frame-structure of video (football sequence)                11

2.2   Block-Matching motion estimation                            13

2.3   1-D and 2-D wavelet decomposition                           15

2.4   Comparison of DCT-based and wavelet-based compression
      schemes                                                     16

2.5   Spatial Orientation Tree                                    17

2.6   JPEG 2000 coding pipeline                                   18

4.1   Runtime analysis of JJ2000 compression for increasing
      image size                                                  36

4.2   Testimages used to evaluate the rate distortion performance. 39

4.3   Rate-distortion performance of JPEG and JPEG 2000.          39

4.4   Time demand.                                                40

4.5   Wireless connections, AES encryption.                       42

4.6   Wired connections (ethernet), AES encryption               42

5.1   VLC encryption results                                      63

5.2   MB permutation results                                      65

5.3   DCT block permutation results                               66

5.4   Motion vector permutation results                           67

5.5   Results of motion vector prediction sign change             68

5.6   Results of motion vector residual sign change               68

5.7   DCT coefficient sign change results                         69

5.8   I-frame sign change results                                 70

5.9   I-frame + I-block sign change results                       70

5.10  DC and AC coefficient mangling results                      71

5.11  DC and AC coefficient mangling results                      72

| 5.12 | DC and AC coefficient mangling results | 72 |
|---|---|---|
| 5.13 | Modified Scan Order (example) | 73 |
| 5.14 | Zig-zag order change results | 74 |
| 5.15 | Compression performance — baseline and progressive JPEG | 79 |
| 5.16 | Lena image; a three level pyramid in HP mode is used with the lowest resolution encrypted | 79 |
| 5.17 | Mandrill image; SS mode is used with DC and first AC coefficient encrypted | 80 |
| 5.18 | Subjective quality of reconstructed Lena image | 82 |
| 5.19 | Images from Fig. 5.18 median filtered (3x3 kernel) and blurred (5x5 filter). | 83 |
| 5.20 | Compression performance, Lena image 512 x 512 pixels | 86 |
| 5.21 | Reconstruction using random filters | 89 |
| 5.22 | Reconstructed image where the heuristic failed at the finest level of decomposition | 89 |
| 5.23 | Reconstructed image where the heuristic failed at 3 out of 5 levels | 89 |
| 5.24 | Quality of JPEG 2000 compression | 91 |
| 5.25 | Attack against a 1-D parameter scheme | 92 |
| 5.26 | Quality of attacked images | 93 |
| 5.27 | Attack against a 2-D parameter scheme | 94 |
| 5.28 | Quality of attacked images | 95 |
| 5.29 | Quality values for $K = 0$. | 97 |
| 5.30 | Parameterised biorthogonal 4/8 filters. | 98 |
| 5.31 | Frequency response | 98 |
| 5.32 | minimum and maximum level of decomposition influencing the quality | 100 |
| 5.33 | Various weight factors for the decomposition decision | 101 |
| 5.34 | All parameters of figures 5.32(a), 5.32(b), 5.33(a), 5.33(b) in one plot | 102 |
| 5.35 | Variance for increasing number of coefficients | 104 |
| 5.36 | Reconstruction using a wrong decomposition tree | 105 |
| 5.37 | Comparison of selective encryption | 110 |
| 5.38 | Angiogram: Comparison of selective encryption | 110 |
| 5.39 | Comparison of selective encryption | 111 |
| 5.40 | Comparison of selective encryption | 112 |

5.41    Angiogram: PSNR of reconstructed images after re-
        placement attack                                         113
5.42    PSNR of reconstructed images after replacement attack    113
5.43    Visual quality of reconstructed Angiogram after replacement  114
5.44    Visual quality of reconstructed Lena after replacement attack  115
5.45    Baker Map (1/2,1/2).                                      116
5.46    Baker Map (1/2,1/2) applied to Lena.                      118
5.47    Visual examples for selective bitplane encryption, di-
        rect reconstruction.                                     119
5.48    Further visual examples for selective bitplane encryption.  120
5.49    Visual examples for encryption of MSB and one addi-
        tional bitplane.                                         121
5.50    Visual examples for the efficiency of the Replacement Attack.  122
5.51    MSB of the Lena image and reconstructed Bitplane.        123
5.52    Combination of two half-images after Reconstruction Attack.  124
5.53    Example for leaf ordering I and II.                       125

# List of Tables

4.1  Number of basic operations for AES encryption  35

4.2  Magnitude order of operations for wavelet transform  35

4.3  Numbers of instructions for wavelet decompositions  36

5.1  Overall assessment of the Zig-zag Permutation Algorithm  49

5.2  Overall assessment of Frequency-band Coefficient Shuffling  49

5.3  Overall assessment of Scalable Coefficient Encryption (in coefficient domain)  50

5.4  Overall assessment of Coefficient Sign Bit Encryption  51

5.5  Overall assessment of Secret Fourier Transform Domain  51

5.6  Overall assessment of Secret Entropy Encoding  52

5.7  Overall assessment of Header Encryption  52

5.8  Overall assessment of Permutations applied at the bit-stream level  54

5.9  Overall assessment of One-time pad VEA  56

5.10  Overall assessment of Byte Encryption  56

5.11  Overall assessment of VLC Codeword encryption  57

5.12  Overall assessment of I-frame Encryption  59

5.13  Overall assessment of Motion Vector Encryption  60

5.14  Objective quality (PSNR in dB) of reconstructed images  81

5.15  Overall assessment of Coefficient Selective Bit Encryption  84

5.16  JPEG 2000/SPIHT: all subbands permuted, max. observed file size increase at a medium compression rate ranging from 25 up to 45  86

5.17  Overall assessment of Coefficient Permutation  87

5.18    Overall assessment of Coefficient Block Permutation
        and Rotation                                                    88
5.19    Overall assessment of Secret Wavelet Filters                    90
5.20    Overall assessment of Secret Wavelet Filters: Parametri-
        sation Approach                                                 99
5.21    Overall assessment of Secret Subband Structures               107
5.22    Overall assessment of SPIHT Encryption                        108
5.23    Overall assessment of JPEG 2000 Encryption                    114
5.24    Overall assessment of Permutations                            116
5.25    Overall assessment of Chaotic Encryption                      117
5.26    PSNR of images after direct reconstruction                    120
5.27    Number of runs consisting of 5 identical bits                 121
5.28    Overall assessment of Bitplane Encryption                     124
5.29    Overall assessment of Quadtree Encryption                     126
5.30    Overall assessment of Encrypting Fractal Encoded Data         126
5.31    Overall assessment of the Virtual Image Cryptosystem          127

# Preface

Contrasting to classical encryption, security may not be the most important aim for an encryption system for images and videos. Depending on the type of application, other properties (like speed or bitstream compliance after encryption) might be equally important as well. As an example, the terms "soft encryption" or "selective encryption" are sometimes used as opposed to classical "hard" encryption schemes like full AES encryption in this context. Such schemes do not strive for maximum security and trade off security for computational complexity. They are designed to protect multimedia content and fulfil the security requirements for a particular multimedia application. For example, real-time encryption for an entire video stream using classical ciphers requires much computation time due to the large amounts of data involved, on the other hand many multimedia applications require security on a much lower level (e.g. TV broadcasting) or should protect their data just for a short period of time (e.g. news broadcast). Therefore, the search for fast encryption procedures specifically tailored to the target environment is mandatory for multimedia security applications. The fields of interest to deploy such solutions span from digital rights management (DRM) schemes to secured personal communication.

Being the first monograph exclusively devoted to image and video encryption systems, this book provides a unified overview of techniques for the encryption of visual data, ranging from commercial applications in the entertainment industry (like DVD or Pay-TV DVB) to more research oriented topics and recently published material. To serve this purpose, we discuss and evaluate different techniques from a unified viewpoint, we provide an extensive bibliography of material related to these topics, and we experimentally compare different systems proposed in the literature and in commercial systems. Several techniques described in this book can be tested online, please refer to http://www.ganesh.org/book/. The cover shows images of the authors which have been encrypted in varying strength using techniques described in section 1.3.8 (chapter 5) in this book.

The authors are members of the virtual laboratory "WAVILA" of the European Network of Excellence ECRYPT, which focuses on watermarking technologies and related DRM issues. National projects financed by the Austrian Science Fund have been supporting the work in the multimedia security area. Being affiliated with the Department of Scientific Computing at Salzburg University, Austria, the authors work in the Multimedia Signal Processing and Security research group, which will be organising as well the 2005 IFIP Communications and Multimedia Security Conference CMS 2005 and an associated summerschool. For more informations, please refer to the website of our group at http://www.scicomp.sbg.ac.at/research/multimedia.html or at http://www.ganesh.org/.

# Acknowledgments

This work has been partially funded by the Austrian Science Fund FWF, in the context of projects no. 13732 and 15170. Parts of the text are copyrighted material. Please refer to the corresponding appendix to obtain detailed information.

# Chapter 1

# INTRODUCTION

Huge amounts of digital visual data are stored on different media and exchanged over various sorts of networks nowadays. Often, these visual data contain private or confidential informations or are associated with financial interests. As a consequence, techniques are required to provide security functionalities like privacy, integrity, or authentication especially suited for these data types. A relatively new field, denoted "Multimedia Security", is aimed towards these emerging technologies and applications.

Several dedicated international meetings have emerged as a forum to present and discuss recent developments in this field, among them "Security, Steganography, and Watermarking of Multimedia Contents" (organised in the framework of SPIE's annual Electronic Imaging Symposium in San Jose) as the most important one. Further important meetings are "Communications and Multimedia Security (CMS)" (annually organised in the framework of IFIP's TC6 and TC11) and the "ACM Multimedia Security Workshop". Additionally, a significant amount of scientific journal special issues has been devoted recently to topics in multimedia security (e.g. ACM/Springer Multimedia Systems, IEEE Transactions on Signal Processing supplement on Secure Media, Signal Processing, EURASIP Applied Signal Processing, ...). The first comprehensive textbook covering this field, the "Multimedia Security Handbook" [54] is published in autumn 2004.

Besides watermarking, steganography, and techniques for assessing data integrity and authenticity, providing confidentiality and privacy for visual data is among the most important topics in the area of multimedia security, applications range from digital rights management (DVD, DVB and pay-TV) to secured personal communications (e.g., encrypted video conferencing). In the following we give some concrete examples of applications which require some type of encryption support to achieve the desired respective functionalities:

**Telemedicine** The organisation of todays health systems often suffers from the fact that different doctors do not have access to each others patient data. The enormous waste of resources for multiple examinations, analyses, and medical check-ups is an immediate consequence. In particular, multiple acquisition of almost identical medical image data and loss of former data of this type has to be avoided to save resources and to provide a time-contiguous medical report for each patient. A solution to these problems is to create a distributed database infrastructure where each doctor has electronic access to all existing medical data related to a patient, in particular to all medical image data acquired over the years. Additionally, many medical professionals are convinced that the future of health care will be shaped by teleradiology and technologies such as telemedicine in general. These facts show very clearly that there is urgent need to provide and protect the confidentiality of patient related medical image data when stored in databases and transmitted over networks of any kind.

**Video Conferencing** In todays communication systems often visual data is involved in order to augment the more traditional purely audio-based systems. Whereas video conferencing (VC) has been around to serve such purposes for quite a while and is conducted on personal computers over computer networks, video telephony is a technology that has been emerging quite recently in the area of mobile cell phone technology. Earlier attempts to marketise videophones operating over traditional phone lines (e.g. in France) have not been very successful. No matter which technology supports this kind of communication application, the range of possible content exchanged is very wide and may include personal communication among friends to chat about recent developments in their respective relationships as well as video conferences between companies to discuss their brand-new product placement strategies for the next three years. In any case, each scenario requires the content to be protected from potential eavesdroppers for obvious reasons.

**Surveillance** The necessary protection of public life from terroristic or criminal acts has caused a tremendous increase of surveillance systems which mostly record and store visual data. Among numerous applications, consider the surveillance of public spaces (like airports or railway stations) and casino-gambling halls. Whereas in the first case the aim is to identify suspicious criminal persons and/or acts, the second application aims at identifying gamblers who try to cheat or are no longer allowed to gamble in that specific casino. In both cases, the information recorded may contain critical private informations of the persons recorded and need to be protected from unauthorised viewers in order to maintain basic citizens' rights. This has to be accomplished during two stages of the surveillance application: first, during transmission from the cameras to the recording site (e.g. over a firewire or even wireless link), and second when recording the data onto the storage media.

**VOD** Video on demand (VOD) is an entertainment application where movies are transmitted from a VOD server to a client after this has been requested by the client, usually video cassette recorder (VCR) functionalities like fast forward or fast backward are assumed (or provided) additionally. The clients' terminals to view the transmitted material may be very heterogeneous in terms of hardware capabilities and network links ranging from a video cell phone to a HDTV station connected to a high speed fibre network. To have access to the video server, the clients have to pay a subscription rate on a monthly basis or on a pay-per-view basis. In any case, in order to secure the revenue for the investments of the VOD company, the transmitted movies have to be secured during transmission in order to protect them from non-paying eavesdropping "clients", and additionally, some means are required to disable a legitimate client to pass over the movies to a non-paying friend or, even worse, to record the movies, burn them onto DVD and sell these products in large quantities (see below). Whereas the first stage (i.e. transmission to the client) may be secured by using cryptography only, some additional means of protection (e.g. like watermarking or fingerprinting) are required to really provide the desired functionalities as we shall see below.

**DVD** The digital versatile disc (DVD) is a storage medium which overcomes the limitations of the CD-ROM in terms of capacity and is mostly used to store and distribute MPEG,MPEG-2 movies and is currently replacing the video cassette in many fields due to its much better quality and much better functionality (except for copying). In order to secure the revenue stream to the content owners and DVD producers the concept of trusted hardware is used: the DVD can be played only on hardware licensed by the DVD consortium, which should disable users from freely copying, distributing, or even reselling recorded DVDs. The concept of trusted hardware is implemented by encryption, i.e. only licensed players or recorders should have the knowledge about necessary keys and algorithms to decode a movie stored on DVD properly. Note that one problem is that if an attacker is successful in decrypting a movie once (not entirely impossible after the crack of the DVD crypto algorithm CSS) or in intercepting the movie when sent from the player to the display in some way (by defeating or circumventing the digital transmission control protocol DTCP) the movie can be distributed freely without any possibility to control or track the copies. Therefore, additional protection means are required in addition to encryption (as already indicated above).

**Pay-TV News** Free-TV is financed via commercials (everywhere) and/or via governmentally imposed, tax-like payments (like e.g. in Austria where everybody who owns a TV-set has to pay those fees no matter if he watches federal TV channels or not). Contrasting to that, Pay-TV is financed by the subscription payments of the clients. As a consequence, only clients having payed their subscription fees should be able to consume Pay-TV channels. This is usually accomplished by encryption of the broadcasted content and decryption in the clients' set-top box, involving some sort of smartcard technology. Whereas the same considerations apply as in the case of VOD with respect to protecting the content during transmission, there is hardly any threat with respect to reselling news content to any other parties since news data loose their value very quickly.

Of course there exist many more applications involving visual data requiring some sort of encryption support, however, we will use these (arbitrary but often discussed) examples to investigate the different requirements on privacy and confidentiality support and the desired properties of the corresponding cryptographic systems. The classical cryptographic approach to handle these different applications is to select a cipher which is proven to be secure and to encrypt the data accordingly, no matter which type of data is processed or in which environment the application is settled. There is a wide variety of encryption techniques out of which an application developer can choose from, including stream ciphers, block ciphers in several modes, symmetric algorithms, public-key algorithms, and many more. All these encryption algorithms have been designed to provide the highest possible level of security while trying to keep the computational load as low as possible, they differ as well with respect to key management and their respective suitability for hardware implementations. An important question is whether the flexibility provided by the different encryption systems is high enough to satisfy the requirements of the given examples and additionally, whether all other properties suit the needs of the application examples. In order to be able to answer these questions, we will discuss the respective requirements and desired properties in some detail.

- **Security**: The required level of security obviously differs a lot among the six given examples. The first group of examples (Telemedicine, VC, Surveillance) is more concerned with basic citizens' rights and protecting telecommunication acts, whereas the second group of applications (VOD, DVD, Pay-TV News) comes from the area of multimedia entertainment where the main concern is the revenue stream of the content owners. Based on this categorisation of applications, one may immediately derive that the first group of applications requires a higher level of security as compared to the second one. While the entertainment industry would not agree to this statement at first sight, "level of security" is not meant in the classical cryptographic sense. Whereas the information content is critical and has therefore to be protected in the case of the first application group this is not the case for the entertainment applications. Here, it is mostly sufficient and acceptable to degrade the quality to an extent that an illegitimate user is not interested to view the material. In certain applications, this situation is even more desirable as compared to "classical encryption" since users might become interested to get access to the full quality when confronted with encrypted but intelligible material. Another important issue is the question how long encrypted visual data has to withstand possible attacks. Again, the first application group has higher requirements as the second one, where one could possibly state that VOD and DVD movies have to be protected only as long as they are relatively new. An extreme case are Pay-TV News where the data loses its value after some hours already. On the other hand it is of course **not** true that entertainment applications do require a much lower "classical" security level in general – a possible argument might be that it does not matter for the revenue stream if some hundred specialists worldwide are able to decipher encrypted entertainment content (since their share of the entire payments is negligible). This is not true for the following reasons:

- As we have learned from peer-to-peer music distribution networks efficient techniques exist to transport digital media data to a large number of possible clients over the internet at low cost. Having the ever increasing network bandwidth in mind, peer-to-peer video distribution is currently taking off and might soon become a threat to the revenue of content owner as it is already the case for audio.

- As we have learned from attacks against DVD CSS and Pay-TV systems, the internet is a good means to distribute key data, decryption software, or even descriptions how to build pirate smartcards.

- With the availability of writable DVDs a medium is at disposal to distribute once cracked entertainment material over classical distribution channels.

As a consequence, it is clear that also for entertainment applications even if it may be acceptable to only degrade the material, this degradation must not be reversible. This excludes encryption schemes relying on weak cryptographic systems from being applied in this area. As long as there are no other restrictions (e.g. as imposed by complexity or data format restrictions, see below), security must not be sacrificed.

- **Speed**: There is one significant difference between the encryption of visual data and the encryption of data encryption is classically applied to (e.g. text data, web documents): visual data is usually much larger, especially in the case of video encryption. Given this fact together with possible timing constraints or real-time requirements it becomes clear that speed might be an important issue. In telemedicine, a certain delay caused the security mechanisms might be acceptable under certain circumstances as well it might be for surveillance. However, when using telemedicine to control remote surgery or the surveillance system is used to trigger actions of security personnel, significant delay is of course not desirable. VC should by performed under real-time constraints of course. DVD encryption is not time critical at all, decryption must not reduce the frame rate of the video when displayed. In the general Pay-TV environment the situation is similar to the DVD case, whereas for on-line live broadcast (as it is the case is News broadcast) encryption has to be done in real-time as well. However, as long as we have point to point connections or a broadcast scenario as in the examples discussed so far, each involved encryption/decryption module has to process a single data stream. The situation is much worse in the VOD application. A video on demand server has to process several streams (corresponding to the clients' requests) concurrently under real-time constraints. Since each stream has to be encrypted separately, this is the "killer application" with respect to speed in the area of visual data encryption.

When discussing speed, two issues that often go hand in hand with execution speed are power consumption and memory requirements. Especially in case the target architecture the encryption has to be performed on is a mobile device low power consumption is crucial for not exhausting the batteries too fast. This could be the case for almost any of the applications discussed except for surveillance. For hardware implementations in general memory is an important cost factor and therefore the corresponding requirements have to be kept to a minimum.

- **Bitstream Compliance**: When encrypting visual data given in some specific data format (e.g. video as MPEG,MPEG-2) with a classical cipher (e.g. AES), the result has nothing to do with an MPEG,MPEG-2 stream any more, it is just an unstructured bitstream. An MPEG player can not decode the video of course, it will crash immediately or, more probably, not even start to process the data due to the lack of header information. While this seems to be desirable from the security viewpoint at first, it becomes clear quickly that causing a common player to be unable to decode has nothing to do with security and provides protection from an unskilled consumer only since a sincere attacker will do much more than just trying to decode encrypted material with a standard decoder. This kind of security is more of the "security by obscurity" type. In order to really assess if the content of a video is protected (and not only the header structures defining how the content has to be interpreted), it can be desirable that the video can be decoded with a standard viewer. Consequently, this requires the encryption to deliver a bitstream which is compliant to the definition of an MPEG video stream. This can be achieved only by keeping the header data intact and by encrypting only the content of the video. Additionally, care has to be taken about the emulation of markers when encrypting video content – the output of the cipher will generally produce symbols which are reserved for bitstream markers of header information in the MPEG definition which will cause a decoder to interpret the following data incorrectly which will cause the viewer to crash eventually.

Assessment of encryption security is not the most important reason for bitstream compliant encryption. Consider the transmission of visual data over a network where the network characteristic (e.g. bandwidth) changes from one segment to the other. The bitrate of the data to be transmitted has to be changed accordingly. Such QoS requirements can be met by modern bitstreams like MPEG,MPEG-4 or JPEG 2000 due to layered or embedded encoding, "older" bitstreams need to be transcoded. In case the bitstream is encrypted in the classical way, it has to be decrypted, the rate adaptation has to be performed, and finally the bitstream is re-encrypted again. All these operations have to be performed at the corresponding network node which raises two problems:

1 The processing overhead at the network node increases and might delay the delivery of the data.

2 The network node must have access to the key data necessary to decrypt the video which is an enormous key management problem.

On the other hand, in case the encryption leads to a compliant bitstream, most adaptation operations can be done directly at the bitstream level without the necessity to decrypt any part of the bitstream. This is simple to implement in the case of layered or embedded bitstreams, if real transcoding has to be performed it is challenging but not impossible to develop techniques for doing this at bitstream level. From our set of example applications, consider accessing a VOD server from a mobile client or using a modem connection in teleradiology as scenarios where this kind of "network-friendliness" is important.

■ **Interference with Compression**: Many applications are mainly retrieval-based, i.e. the visual data is already available in compressed format and has to be retrieved from a storage medium (e.g. VOD, DVD), contrasting to applications where the data is acquired and compressed subsequently. In order to support such retrieval-based applications, it has to be possible to perform the encryption in the compressed domain at bitstream level. Additionally, the bitrate of the visual data in compressed form is lower and therefore the encryption process is faster if applied to compressed data. The relation between compression and encryption will be discussed in more detail in section 3 (chapter 4).

As we have seen, the requirements imposed from the applications side are numerous – high security, fast encryption, fast decryption, bitstream compliance, little power consumption, little memory requirements, no interference with compression – often these requirements can not be met simultaneously and contradict each other:

- High speed vs. high security: As we have seen from the VOD example, real-time encryption while using classical full encryption with a standard cryptographic cipher may be hard to fulfil due to simultaneous requests from many clients. This may be as well the case in the VC application if mobile devices are involved which may not be able to deliver the required processing power to provide full real-time encryption. For low-bitrate applications like GSM or UMTS this has been solved already.

- High speed vs. bitstream compliance and bitstream processing: The easiest way to achieve bitstream compliance is to apply encryption during the compression stage. Since this is not possible in case bitstream processing is mandatory, obtaining bitstream compliance usually requires the bitstream to be parsed and carefully encrypted. Obviously, this contradicts the aim of high speed processing.

- High security vs. bitstream compliance: The best solution from the security viewpoint is to encrypt visual data with a classical cryptographic cipher in a secure operation mode no matter which format is used to represent the data. Bitstream compliant encryption requires the header data to be left intact which means that only small contiguous sets of data are encrypted which leads to a high amount of start up phases which may threaten security.

- No compression interference vs. bitstream compliance: As already mentioned before, the easiest way to achieve bitstream compliance is to apply encryption during the compression stage of visual data. When doing this, interfering with the compression process (especially with the entropy coding stage) can hardly be avoided.

Which of these requirements are more important than others depends on the application. A solution often suggested in the entertainment area is not to stick to absolute security but to trade-off between security and other requirements, usually computational complexity, i.e. speed: Some multimedia applications require just a basic level of security (e.g. TV broadcast), but on the other hand they output large amounts of compressed data in realtime which should be encrypted. Often the content provided by such applications loses its value very fast, like in the case of news broadcasts. As an example, the techniques "soft encryption" or "selective encryption" are sometimes used as opposed to classical "hard" encryption schemes like full AES encryption in this context.

Encryption may have an entirely different purpose as opposed to confidentiality or privacy as required by most applications described above. For example, "transparent" encryption [90] of video data provides low quality visual data for free, for full quality the user has to pay some fee. The additional data to be purchased is available to all users in encrypted form, only the legitimate user obtains a corresponding key. This type of application also necessarily involves encryption techniques, but these techniques do not aim for confidentiality here but facilitate a specific business model for trading visual data.

As a consequence of these different application scenarios with all their specific requirements and properties a large amount of research effort has been done in the last years which resulted in a large number of purely research oriented publications in this field on the one hand. On the other hand, in the area of consumer electronics and standardisation [42, 44] there exist few important products besides many small solutions offering proprietary work, however, their respective success is questionable in terms of security or is subject to future developments:

- Pay-TV: Analog and hybrid Pay-TV encryption systems have been broken due to severe weaknesses of their ciphers (contradicting Kerckhoffs principle all schemes followed the principle "security by obscurity" as it was the case with DVD encryption), reverse engineered smartcards, and by exploiting the internet as a key distribution means. Digital systems relying on DVB distribution have turned out to be much stronger with respect to their cipher but again a web-based key-sharing technique has been established soon threatening the success of the scheme (e.g. against Premiere in Austria and Germany [165]).

- DVD: The concept of trusted hardware did not work out properly when software DVD players entered the scene and finally the secret CSS cipher was broken and decryption software was published on the internet and on the back of T-shirts.

- MPEG IPMP: In the context of MPEG,MPEG-4 and MPEG,MPEG-21 the intellectual property management protocol has been defined to provide a standardised framework for digital rights management (DRM) issues including encryption support. These techniques provide a syntactical framework but no specific techniques have been standardised. Applications making use of these definitions are still yet to come.

- JPSEC: As part 8 of the JPEG 2000 standardisation effort, JPSEC has been defined to provide a standardised framework for digital rights management (DRM) issues including encryption support. As it is the case with MPEG's IPMP, these techniques provide a syntactical framework but no specific techniques have been standardised. Applications making use of these definitions are still yet to come.

The aim of this monograph is to provide a unified overview of techniques for the encryption of images and video data, ranging from commercial applications like DVD or DVB to more research oriented topics and recently published material. To serve this purpose, we discuss and evaluate different techniques from a unified viewpoint, we provide an extensive bibliography of material related to these topics, and we experimentally compare different systems proposed in the literature and in commercial systems.

The organisation of the book is as follows. In order to achieve the goal of a self-contained piece of work to a certain extent, chapters 2 and 3 review the principles of visual data representation and classical encryption techniques, respectively. Chapter 2 focuses on compression techniques and covers standards like JPEG, JPEG 2000, MPEG 1-4, H.26X, but also proprietary solutions of importance with respect to combined compression/encryption like quadtree compression or the wavelet based SPIHT algorithm. Chapter 3 explains the differences between public-key and symmetric cryptography, between block ciphers and stream ciphers, and covers symmetrical encryption algorithms like DES, IDEA, and AES as well as the most important corresponding operation modes (like ECB, CBC, and so on). In chapter 4 we discuss application scenarios for visual data encryption: the terms selective and soft encryption are defined and conditions for the sensible use of these techniques are derived. Subsequently, the relation between compression and encryption is analysed in depth. Chapter 5 is the main part of this work where we describe, analyse, and assess various techniques for encrypting images and videos. In this context, a large amount of experimental data resulting from custom implementations is provided. Finally, chapter 6 summaries the results and provides outlooks to open questions and future issues in the area of image and video encryption.

# Chapter 2

# VISUAL DATA FORMATS

## 1. Image and Video Data

Digital visual data is usually organised in rectangular arrays denoted as frames, the elements of these arrays are denoted as pixels (picture elements). Each pixel is a numerical value, the magnitude of the value specifies the intensity of this pixel. The magnitude of the pixels varies within a predefined range which is classically denoted as "bitdepth", i.e. if the bitdepth is 8 bit, the magnitude of the pixel varies between 0 and $2^8 - 1$ (8 bpp means 8 bits per pixel). Typical examples are binary images (i.e. black and white images) with 1 bpp only or grayvalue images with 8 bpp where the grayvalues vary between 0 and 255.

Colour is defined by using several frames, one for each colour channel. The most prominent example is the RGB representation, where a full resolution frame is devoted to each of the colours red, green, and blue. Colour representations closer to human perception differentiate among luminance and colour channels (e.g. the YUV model).

Video adds a temporal dimension to the purely spatially oriented image data. A video consists of single frames which are temporally ordered one after the other (see Fig. 2.1). A single video frame may again consist of several frames for different colour channels.

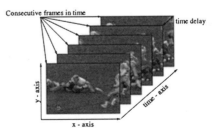

*Figure 2.1.* Frame-structure of video (football sequence)

Visual data constitutes enormous amounts of data to be stored, transmitted, or processed. Therefore, visual data is mostly subjected to compression algorithms after capturing (or digitisation). Two big classes of compression algorithms exist:

- Lossless compression: after having decompressed the data, it is numerically identical to the original values.

- Lossy compression: the decompressed data is an approximation of the original values.

Lossy algorithms achieve much higher compression ratios (i.e. the fraction between original filesize and the size of the compressed file) as compared to the lossless case. However, due to restrictions imposed by some application areas, lossless algorithms are important as well (e.g. in the area of medical imaging lossless compression is mandatory in many countries due to legislative reasons). However, in the multimedia area lossy compression algorithms are more important, the most distinctive classification criterion is whether the underlying integral transform is the discrete cosine transform (DCT) or the wavelet transform.

## 2.    DCT-based Systems

### 2.1    JPEG

The baseline system of the JPEG standard [169, 110] operates on $8 \times 8$ pixels blocks onto which a DCT is applied. The resulting data are quantised using standardised quantisation matrices, subsequently the quantised coefficients are scanned following a zig-zag order (which orders the data in increasing frequency), the resulting vector is Huffman and runlength encoded (see right side of Fig. 2.4).

The JPEG standard also contains an extended system where several progressive modes are defined (see section 1.4.1 (chapter 5)) and a lossless codes which uses not DCT but is entirely DPCM (difference pulse coded modulation) based.

### 2.2    MPEG Video Coding (MPEG-1,2,4)

The main idea of MPEG motion compensated video coding [99, 60] is to use the temporal **and** spatial correlation between frames in a video sequence [153] (Fig. 2.1) for predicting the current frame from previously (de)coded ones. Some frames are compressed in similar manner to JPEG compression, which are random access points to the sequence, these frames are called I-frames. All other frames are predicted from decoded I-frames – in case a bidirectional temporal prediction is done the corresponding frames are denoted B-frames, simple unidirectional prediction leads to P-frames. Since this prediction fails in some regions (e.g. due to occlusion), the residual between this prediction and the current frame being processed is computed and additionally stored after lossy compression. This compression is again similar to JPEG compression but a different quantisation matrix is used.

Because of its simplicity and effectiveness block-matching algorithms are widely used to remove temporal correlation [53]. In block-matching motion compensation, the scene (i.e. video frame) is classically divided into non-overlapping "block" regions. For estimating the motion, each block in the current frame is compared against the blocks in the search area in the reference frame (i.e. previously encoded and decoded frame) and the motion vector $(d_1, d_2)$ corresponding to the best match is returned (see Fig. 2.2). The "best" match of the blocks is identified to be that match giving the minimum mean square error (MSE) of all blocks in search area defined as

$$MSE(d_1, d_2) = \frac{1}{N_1 N_2} \sum_{(n_1, n_2) \in \mathcal{B}} [s_k(n_1, n_2) - \hat{s}_{k-l}(n_1 + d_1, n_2 + d_2)]^2$$

where $\mathcal{B}$ denotes a $N_1 * N_2$ block for a set of candidate motion vectors $(d_1, d_2)$, $s$ is the current frame and $\hat{s}$ the reference frame.

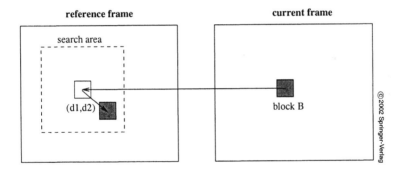

*Figure 2.2.*   Block-Matching motion estimation

The algorithm which visits all blocks in the search area to compute the minimum is called full search. In order to speed up the search process, many techniques have been proposed to reduce the number of candidate blocks. The main idea is to introduce a specific search pattern which is recursively applied at the position of the minimal local error. The most popular algorithm of this type is called "Three Step Search" which reduces the computational amount significantly at the cost of a suboptimal solution (and therefore a residual with slightly more energy). The block giving the minimal error is stored describing the prediction in term of a motion vector which describes the displacement of the block. The collection of all motion vectors of a frame is called motion vector field.

MPEG-1 has been originally defined for storing video on CD-ROM, therefore the data rate and consequently the video quality is rather low. MPEG,MPEG-2 [60] is very similar from the algorithmic viewpoint, however the scope is shifted to TV broadcasting and even HDTV. The quality is much higher as compared to MPEG-1, additionally methodologies have been standardised to enable scalable video streams and error resilience functionalities.

MPEG-4 [40, 124] extends the scope of the MPEG standards series to natural and synthetic (i.e. computer generated) video and provides technologies for interactive video (i.e. object-based video coding). The core compression engine is again similar to MPEG-2 to provide backward compatibility to some extent. Finally, MPEG-4 AVC (also denoted H.264 in the ITU standards series) increases compression efficiency significantly as compared to MPEG-4 video at an enormous computational cost [124].

## 2.3    ITU H.26X Video Conferencing

The ITU series of video conferencing standards is very similar to the MPEG standards, however, there is one fundamental difference: video conferencing has to meet real-time constraints. Therefore, the most expensive part of video coding (i.e. motion compensation) needs to be restricted. As a consequence, H.261 defines no B-frames in contrast to MPEG-1 and H.263 is also less complex as compared to MPEG-2. In particular, H.261 and H.263 offer better quality at low bitrates as compared to their MPEG counterparts. H.261 has been defined to support video conferencing over ISDN, H.263 over PSTN which implies the demand for even lower bitrates in H.263. The latest standard in this series is H.264 which has been designed by the JVT (joint video team) and is identical to MPEG-4 AVC. This algorithm uses a $4 \times 4$ pixels integer transform (which is similar to the DCT) and multi-frame motion compensation. Therefore, this algorithm is very demanding from a computational point of view.

## 3.    Wavelet-based Systems

Image compression methods that use wavelet transforms [154] (which are based on multiresolution analysis – MRA) have been successful in providing high compression ratios while maintaining good image quality, and have proven to be serious competitors to DCT based compression schemes.

A wide variety of wavelet-based image compression schemes have been reported in the literature [62, 86], ranging from first generation systems which are similar to JPEG only replacing the DCT by wavelets to more complex techniques such as vector quantisation in the wavelet domain [7, 26, 10], adaptive transforms [31, 160, 175], and edge-based coding [52]. Second generation wavelet compression schemes try to take advantage of inter subband correlation – the most prominent algorithms in this area are zerotree encoding [135, 81] and hybrid fractal wavelet codecs [142, 30]. In most of these schemes, compression is accomplished by applying a fast wavelet transform to decorrelate the image data, quantising the resulting transform coefficients (this is where the actual lossy compression takes place) and coding the quantised values taking into account the high inter-subband correlations.

The fast wavelet transform (which is used in signal and image processing) can be efficiently implemented by a pair of appropriately designed Quadrature Mirror Filters (QMF). Therefore, wavelet-based image compression can be viewed as a form of subband coding. A 1-D wavelet transform of a signal $s$ is performed by convolving $s$ with both QMF's and downsampling by 2; since $s$ is finite, one must make some choice about what values to pad the extensions with [150]. This operation decomposes the original signal into two frequency-bands (called subbands), which are often denoted as coarse scale approximation (lowpass subband) and detail signal (highpass subband). Then, the same procedure is applied recursively to the coarse scale approximations several times (see Figure 2.3.a).

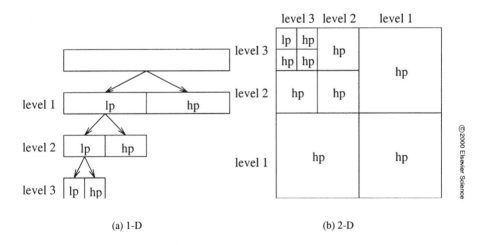

(a) 1-D          (b) 2-D

*Figure 2.3.* 1-D and 2-D wavelet decomposition: lowpass (lp) and highpass (hp) subbands, decomposition levels (level 1 – level 3)

The classical 2-D transform is performed by two separate 1-D transforms along the rows and the columns of the image data, resulting at each decomposition step in a low pass image (the coarse scale approximation) and three detail images (see Figure 2.3.b); for more details see [91].

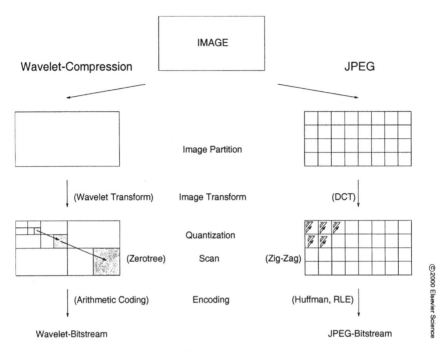

*Figure 2.4.*   Comparison of DCT-based and wavelet-based compression schemes

Fig. 2.4 shows the differences between DCT and wavelet based schemes – whereas the differences are restricted to the transform stage for first generation schemes, also the scan order and entropy encoding is different for second generation systems.

## 3.1    SPIHT

It can be observed that the coefficients calculated by a wavelet decomposition contain a high degree of spatial self similarity across all subbands. By considering this similarity, a more efficient coefficient representation can be obtained which is exploited by all second generation wavelet coding schemes. SPIHT [126] uses a spatial orientation tree which is shown in Figure 2.5. This data structure is very similar to the zerotree structure used by the EZW zerotree algorithm [135], each value in the wavelet multiresolution pyramid is assigned to a node of the tree.

Three lists are used to represent the image information: The LIS (list of insignificant sets), the LIP (list of insignificant pixels), and the LSP (list of significant pixels). The latter list contains the sorted coefficients which are stored. The following algorithm iteratively operates on these lists thereby adding and deleting coefficients $c_{i,j}$ to/from the lists (where $\mu_n$ denotes the number of coefficients which have their most significant bit within bitplane $n$):

1 output $n = \lfloor \log_2 (max_{(i,j)}\{|c_{i,j}|\}) \rfloor$ to the decoder.

2 output $\mu_n$, followed by the pixel coordinates and sign of each of the $\mu_n$ coefficients such that $2^n \leq |c_{i,j}| < 2^{n+1}$ (**sorting pass**);

3 output the $n$-th most significant bit of all the coefficients $|c_{i,j}| \geq 2^{n+1}$ (i.e., those that had their coordinates transmitted in previous sorting passes), in the same order used to send the coordinates (**refinement pass**);

4 decrement $n$ by 1, and go to step 2.

The SPIHT codec generates an embedded bitstream and is optimised for encoding speed. SPIHT is not a standard but a proprietary commercial product which has been the state of the art codec each new image compression system was compared to for several years. The SMAWZ codec [78] used is some sections of this book is a variant of SPIHT which uses bitplanes instead of lists to ease processing and to save memory accesses. Additionally, SMAWZ generalises SPIHT to wavelet packet subband structures and anisotropic wavelet decomposition schemes.

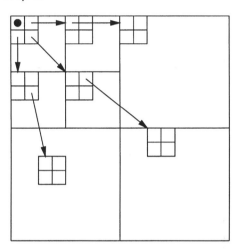

*Figure 2.5.* Spatial Orientation Tree

## 3.2 JPEG 2000

The JPEG 2000 image coding standard [152] is based on a scheme originally proposed by Taubman and known as EBCOT ("Embedded Block Coding with Optimised Truncation" [151]). The major difference between previously proposed wavelet-based image compression algorithms such as EZW or SPIHT (see [154]) is that EBCOT as well as JPEG 2000 operate on independent, non-overlapping blocks which are coded in several bit layers to create an embedded, scalable bitstream. Instead of zerotrees, the JPEG 2000 scheme depends on a per-block quad-tree structure since the strictly independent block coding strategy precludes structures across subbands or even code-blocks. These independent code-blocks are passed down the "coding pipeline" shown in Fig.

2.6 and generate separate bitstreams (Tier-1 coding). Transmitting each bit layer corresponds to a certain distortion level. The partitioning of the available bit budget between the code-blocks and layers ("truncation points") is determined using a sophisticated optimisation strategy for optimal rate/distortion performance (Tier-2 coding).

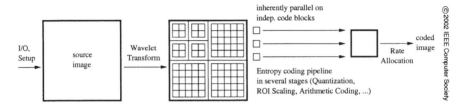

*Figure 2.6.*    JPEG 2000 coding pipeline

The main design goals behind EBCOT and JPEG 2000 are versatility and flexibility which are achieved to a large extent by the independent processing and coding of image blocks [23], and of course to provide a codec with a better rate-distortion performance than the widely used JPEG, especially at lower bitrates. The default for JPEG 2000 is to perform a five-level wavelet decomposition with 7/9-biorthogonal filters and then segment the transformed image into non-overlapping code-blocks of no more than 4096 coefficients which are passed down the coding pipeline.

Two JPEG 2000 reference implementations are available online: the JJ2000 codec (see `http://jj2000.epfl.ch`) implemented in JAVA and the Jasper C codec (see `http://www.ece.ubc.ca/~madams`).

## 4.    Further Techniques

### 4.1    Quadtrees

Quadtree compression partitions the visual data into a structural part (the quadtree structure) and colour information (the leave values). The quadtree structure shows the location and size of each homogeneous region, the colour information represents the intensity of the corresponding region. The generation of the quadtree follows the splitting strategy well known from the area of image segmentation. Quadtree image compression comes in lossless as well in lossy flavour, the lossy variant is obtained in case the homogeneity criterion is less stringent. This technique is not competitive from the rate distortion efficiency viewpoint, but it is much faster than any transform based compression technique.

## 4.2 Fractal Coding

Fractal image compression [47, 11] exploits similarities within images. These similarities are described by a contractive transformation of the image whose fixed point is close to the image itself. The image transformation consists of block transformations which approximate smaller parts of the image by larger ones. The smaller parts are called ranges and the larger ones domains. All ranges together (range-pool) form a partition of the image. Often an adaptive quadtree partition is applied to the image. The domains can be selected freely within the image and may overlap (domain-pool). For each range an appropriate domain must be found. If no appropriate domain can be found (according to a certain error measure and a tolerance) the range blocks are split which reduces the compression efficiency.

Although fractal compression exhibits promising properties (like e.g. fractal interpolation and resolution independent decoding) the encoding complexity turned out to be prohibitive for successful employment of the technique. Additionally, fractal coding has never reached the rate distortion performance of second generation wavelet codecs.

## 4.3 Vector Quantisation

Vector quantisation [3] exploits similarities between image blocks and an external codebook. The image to be encoded is tiled into smaller image blocks which are compared against equally sized blocks in an external codebook. For each image block the most similar codebook block is identified and the corresponding index is recorded. From the algorithmic viewpoint, the process is similar to fractal coding, therefore fractal coding is sometimes referred to as vector quantisation with internal codebook. Similar to fractal coding, the encoding process involves a search for an optimal block match and is rather costly, whereas the decoding process in the case of vector quantisation is even faster since it is a simple lookup table operation.

## 4.4 Lossless Formats: JBIG, GIF, PNG

Whereas most lossy compression techniques combine several algorithms (e.g., transformation, quantisation, coding), lossless techniques often employ a single compression algorithm in rather pure form. Lossless JPEG as described before employs a DPCM codec. GIF and PNG both use dictionary coding as the underlying technique – LZW coding in the case of GIF and LZSS coding in the case of PNG. JBIG uses context-based binary arithmetic coding for compressing bitplanes. For some details on these lossless compression techniques see [61].

Chapter 3

# CRYPTOGRAPHY PRIMER

## 1. Introduction, Terminology

Cryptography, cryptanalysis (sometimes also written cryptoanalysis), cryptology: What is this all about? Do these words mean the same? Let us first turn towards the origin of these words:

**cryptos:** greek for *hidden*

**graphos:** greek for *to write or draw*

**logos:** greek for *word, reason or discourse*

**analysis:** originating from the the greek "analusis", *the division of a physical or abstract whole into its constituent parts to examine or determine their relationship or value*

Cryptologists differentiate between the three terms:

**cryptography:** is the study of mathematical techniques related to aspects of information security such as confidentiality, data integrity, entity authentication, and data origin authentication (see [96, p.4]).

**cryptanalysis:** is the study of mathematical techniques for attempting to defeat cryptographic techniques, and more generally, information security services (see [96, p.15]).

**cryptology:** is the study of cryptography and cryptanalysis.

For many centuries cryptology was an art practised in black chambers, just some decades ago it became science.

A message readable by humans or computers is usually called *plaintext*. During a transformation called *encryption* the *ciphertext* is generated out of the plaintext. The intention is that this ciphertext cannot by deciphered except by the legitimate recipient. The recipient performs the inverse transformation called *decryption* to recreate the original plaintext.

The main purpose of cryptography is to provide means to create *confidentiality*, to keep data secret. Besides that cryptography gives us *authentication*, the ability to prove the sender and not someone else sent a message, *integrity*, the inability to modify a message without detection and *nonrepudiation*, the inability to falsely deny that the sender sent the message.

Many different variants to encrypt data have been invented, these algorithms are also called *ciphers*. Modern cryptography relies on the Kerckhoff Principle [70]: One must assume that all details about the cipher are known to the enemy, the exact algorithm and all its inner workings, except one small piece of data called *key*. The output of the cipher should depend solely on the key (and of course on the input data). Modern ciphers should withstand all attacks to deduct the key from some other data, even in such extreme cases when the attacker can choose the input data for the "black box" cipher+key and subsequently read the output data. Later we will explain the different variants of attacks in more detail.

**The family of Alice and Bob.**     When cryptologists talk about different scenarios of encryption methods and possible attacks they call the involved parties by distinct names with predefined roles: Starting with the alphabet are Alice and Bob, two parties who want to communicate in a secure manner. What makes things more interesting is that in most scenarios both do not know each other. When more people are necessary Carol and Dave appear. Eve is an evil eavesdropper who engages just in passive means to illegitimately acquire some information. Mallory is her malicious counterpart who actively inserts or modifies data on the way between Alice and Bob. Trent is a person who is trusted by all involved parties. In some occasions more people are required, according to Schneier [131] the warden Walter, the prover Peggy and the verifier Victor.

## 2.     Secret key vs. Public key Cryptography

Modern cryptography gives us two classes of encryption methods:

**symmetric ciphers:** the family of secret-key cryptography. This is the traditional way of secret communications: both the sender and the receiver agree on a single key for their communication, the key is used to encrypt and to decrypt the data. Typical key sizes are 56 bits (DES), 64 bits (CAST or Blowfish), 128 bits (IDEA, AES), 192 and 256 bits (both AES).

**asymmetric ciphers:** also called public-key cryptography. In this case two different keys are involved, they are related by some mathematical property. Everybody who is in possession of the public key can encrypt data, but cannot decrypt it, just the person holding the secret key can decrypt this data. Typical key lengths are 768, 1024, 2048 bits (RSA, ElGamal). Keys based on elliptical curves have typical lengths of 150 to 200 bits. Key lengths of different algorithms cannot be compared directly because they rely on different mathematical properties, e.g. some researchers say that 170 bits for elliptical curves provide roughly the same security as 1024 bits for RSA.

Both classes have their advantages and disadvantages. Symmetric ciphers are fast, but every party must keep the key absolutely secret, this becomes more dangerous with an increasing number of involved parties. Additionally, for each pair of persons who want to communicate a different key must be agreed upon. This makes key management very cumbersome. Asymmetric ciphers are computationally much more expensive, but the public key can be distributed to every one, just one person has to guard the secret part of the key. Besides that there is a multitude of hints that asymmetric ciphers are practically secure but a mathematical proof for any individual cipher is still missing.

## 3. Block Ciphers

Secret-key ciphers can be partitioned into two groups: block ciphers and stream ciphers. The unit of operation is a block of data, its size depends on the actual cipher, common values are 64 and 128 bits of data, sometimes larger, older ciphers use smaller blocks, whereas modern ciphers prefer larger block sizes. Block ciphers process one block of input data, transform it to another block of output data (based on some key) of the same size, then proceed to the next block. Stream ciphers operate on a continuous stream of undetermined size, some ciphers process the data bit after bit, other ciphers process the data byte-wise.

One advantage of a block cipher is their speed. Modern processors possess large register banks with long registers, they can process large portions of such blocks at once with single statements. Additionally it is computationally very expensive to mount an exhaustive attack on blocks with size 64 or even 128 bits, compared to blocks of 8 bits: as each bit in the original data influences the output the number of possible outputs doubles with every bit. Therefore the probability of correctly "guessing" the plaintext data is much lower with larger block lengths.

The drawback is that the underlying data must be organised in chunks which have the size of the encryption blocks. If this is not the case, the data must be padded with some additional data. An example for this would be an encrypted remote login session where the user types the keys on the local keyboard and transmits them over some network to the remote host: one byte typed by the user and 7 bytes added for padding is not efficient of course. Sometimes padding is not possible at all. Imagine an application using a record set of data with fixed lengths, when one wants to encrypt pieces of data smaller then the blocksize, it must be padded, but the result does not fit into the record set any more.

## 3.1    sidestep: XOR

In the following we will often refer to the XOR-operation $\oplus$. It is very popular in cryptology because it is its own inverse function:

| input 1 | input 2 | XOR output |
|---------|---------|------------|
| 0 | 0 | 0 |
| 0 | 1 | 1 |
| 1 | 0 | 1 |
| 1 | 1 | 0 |

Given a plaintext bitstream $T$ and some secret bitstream $S$ then the application of the bitwise XOR-operation gives $C = T \oplus S$. The inverse operation to recompute the original is $T' = C \oplus S = (T \oplus S) \oplus S = T \oplus (S \oplus S) = T \oplus 0 = T$, therefore $T' = T$. These bitstreams $T$, $S$ and $C$ can be fixed length blocks of bits or a continuous stream of bits. The basic principle is the same: at a certain point during encryption a common secret stream is XORed with the input data, and during decryption the same secret stream is XORed again to produce the original plaintext. Sometimes XOR is also referred to as "addition modulo 2".

## 3.2    Operation Modes for Block Ciphers

Block ciphers can be deployed in different so-called "Operation Modes". Depending on external requirements or threats to avoid a suitable mode should be chosen. The most common modes are:

**ECB = electronic codebook mode:** the most obvious mode. Here each block of data is encrypted/decrypted completely independent of all data before or after this block. This has the advantage that encryption of multiple blocks in parallel is possible, transmission errors are confined to the current block. The disadvantage is that this mode is susceptible for replay attacks or traffic analysis: a block containing constant data is encrypted every time to the same cipher block provided the same key is used.

**CBC = cipher block chaining mode:** This mode can be a solution against the replay attacks on the ECB mode. Here the output (the ciphertext) of the previous block and the plaintext of the current block are XOR-ed and subsequently encrypted and transmitted/stored. The output of the current block is used for the XOR-operation with the next plaintext block. The decryption works in reverse order: the current ciphertext block is decrypted, the result XOR-ed with the previous ciphertext block, the result is the original plaintext block. A careful reader might have noticed that there is a problem at the beginning, to solve this a dummy block must be transmitted first to start the chain, this block is also called "initialisation vector" (IV). Transmission errors have a slightly larger impact, a flipped bit leads to completely different plaintext version of the current block (as in ECB), and it changes a single bit of plaintext in the next block.

**CFB = cipher feedback mode:** This mode and the following modes have been invented to transform a block cipher into a stream cipher. These modes can be used when data must be encrypted with a size less than the block length. Again, at the beginning an initialisation vector is used, it is put into a shift register (in the following we assume that it shifts from right to left). The contents of this register is encrypted, the left-most $n$ bits are used for an XOR-operation with plaintext of size $n$. The resulting cipher data (again size $n$) is sent or stored and additionally put back into the shift register on the right side. The decryption operation is almost identical to the encryption operation: it is initialised with the same IV. The received cipher data of size $n$ is put into the shift register, its contents encrypted and the left-most $n$ bits of its output XOR-ed with the just-received cipher data. Care must be taken that the IV is unique for every message, but there are no absolute requirements to keep it secret.

**OFB = output feedback mode:** is similar to CFB. Whereas in CFB-mode the result of the XOR-function is put back into the shift register, in OFB the loop does not involve data from a user, the feedback-loop comprises just the shift register and the encryption function: the result of the encryption function is fed back to the shift register. This has the advantage that the key stream can be computed independently of the data that must be encrypted.

**CTR = counter mode:** Similar to OFB, but here no shift register is used. Instead a counter value is used as the input to encryption function, after each encryption the counter is changed, usually it is incremented by one. An advantage of this mode is that random access mode to some data is possible, without the drawbacks of ECB. An example application is described in RFC 3686 ([63]).

## 3.3 DES and triple-DES

DES and its variant triple-DES are example algorithms for block ciphers, and probably the most widely used block ciphers. DES is a standard developed first at IBM, subsequently modified and finally published by the US NIST (see

[101]). DES uses blocks which contain 64 bits and keys with a length of 56 bits. DES performs 16 rounds of substitution (with given S-boxes) and permutation (with given P-boxes).

64-bit blocks and 56-bit keys were sufficient to provide enough practical security at the time of its publication (1975) as well as for the next years. Its validity has been prolonged several times by NIST until it became obvious that brute-force cracking was feasible. A public brute-force attempt was performed by the EFF in 1998: they showed that it is possible to break a cipher by brute-force with an investment of just 200000 US$ (see [49]). Moores law can be applied here, this means that every 18 months the expected duration can be divided by 2 (with fixed costs), or that the costs can be divided by 2 (with fixed time). This constituted a problem since many organisations relied on DES.

Countermeasures have been taken, even before this public demonstration: DES can be extended to triple-DES where any plaintext block was mangled three times by the DES algorithm instead of just one time. Depending on the actual implementation this gave keys with a length of 2*56 or 3*56 bits. This is still sufficient secure for most applications, but triple-DES has a drawback: it is very slow when compared to other ciphers of similar strength. The reason for this is that DES was designed in the early 1970ies with 4-bit processors in mind, at this time top-of-the-line, but the algorithm does not perform too good on current 32-bit CPUs. And then triple the time for triple-DES. So another countermeasure was applied: establish a different cipher as a new standard. This leads to AES, the Advanced Encryption Standard.

## 3.4    AES

AES is the successor of DES, the winner of a contest organised by NIST and subsequently published as standard (see [102]). NIST set up a list of rules, besides the security guidelines e.g. that it should perform well on very different kind of hardware ranging from 8-bit CPUs on smartcard to modern 64-bit server CPUs. This new algorithm uses blocks of size 128 bits, and it allows keys with 128, 192 or 256 bit length. The winner algorithm was designed by two Belgian cryptologists, Joan Daemen and Vincent Rijmen, with their algorithm "Rijndael", which is based on Galois Field theory.

At the NIST website you can find an outdated info page which NIST keeps deliberately for users to be able to see historic information[1], it provides a FAQ page[2], and the actual standard can be obtained from http://csrc.nist.gov/publications/fips/fips197/fips-197.pdf. Additional information can be found on the Rijndael Fan Page at http://www.rijndael.com/ .

The algorithm performs 10, 12 or 14 rounds, the number of round depends on the size of the key. In each round four functions for perturbation of the input data are called, their names are SubBytes(), ShiftRows(), MixColumns(), and AddRoundKey(). The creators of the AES cipher explain their algorithm in several publications: [27–29].

Since a replacement for DES has been established NIST currently proposes to withdraw DES as a standard, just keeping it in the triple-DES variant[103].

## 3.5  Other Blockciphers

Of course there are more block ciphers than the two by NIST, many people and organisations try to invent secure ciphers. The general problem with any cipher is that it must be tested and tried to get an impression of its security. The best way would be to prove that a cipher is secure, but that is difficult, and does not help about yet to be discovered attacks.

Some other ciphers which are considered secure are the competitors in the AES challenge in round $2^3$: MARS, RC6, Serpent, Twofish. Another cipher is IDEA, invented by Ascom, now a company called MediaCrypt is in charge of this cipher[4]. Some years ago the NSA created a classified cipher called Skipjack, later it became declassified and now the information is online at http://csrc.nist.gov/CryptoToolkit/skipjack/skipjack-kea.htm. UMTS cell phones use another block algorithm, KASUMI [1], this block cipher is used for both the confidentiality function f8 and the integrity function f9 [2]. And there are a lot more ciphers which are more or less secure...

## 4.  Stream Ciphers

Stream ciphers are different to block ciphers, they do not transform blocks of data to another block of data. Instead, based on a key a (theoretically infinite length) key stream is generated, like a pseudo-random number generator. This key stream is used to XOR it with the plain text. The decryption operation is identical to the encryption operation.

Many stream ciphers are based on linear feedback shift registers (LFSR) because of the ease of implementation in hardware. The downside is that in general they are insecure. Examples for LFSR ciphers are the first version of A5, the algorithm used in GSM phones (currently there are three versions A5/1 - A5/3), or the cipher which encrypts the GPS signal.

Other ciphers which rely on non-linear or clock-controlled generators (an example for the latter is the shrinking generator) seem to perform better than the linear generators. A commercial example for a stream cipher is RC4 which is officially a trade secret but many implementations have been published which are said to interoperate with the original. RC4 has some minor weaknesses, some bits of the key leak into the first bits of the encrypted stream, an overview of publications about RC4 is available on the WWW[5]. RC4 comes with many products, currently the most popular is the WEP (wired equivalent protocol) encryption used in wireless LAN devices, it contains RC4 with a 40 bit key. WEP incorporates the weaknesses of RC4 and has some of its own, the short key does not help either. Another approach to generate a stream cipher is to use a cryptographically strong pseudo random number (or bit) generator like Blum-Blum-Shub.

## 4.1   One Time Pad — OTP

The OTP is different to all other stream ciphers because there is a requirement that the key stream must not be repeated, i.e. all kind of pseudo-random number generators are not qualified for OTP. It can be proved that this method is ultimately secure, but there are some other problems associated with it: key distribution and randomness. Since the key must be at least as long as the plaintext Alice and Bob must exchange the same amount of key data before they exchange this amount of encrypted message. The key must be absolutely random, therefore generators which are based solely on software cannot be used, it is necessary to use some source of entropy outside of a computer, like atomic decay and radiation.

## 5.    Hybrid Algorithms, some Applications

As stated before public key algorithms are slow, but are to be preferred because of the advantages in key distribution, especially when parties want to communicate who do not know each other beforehand. On the other hand one does not want to miss the main advantage of the symmetric secret key algorithms: speed. The solution is to use the best of both worlds.

## 5.1   PGP

A long established example is PGP [9, 19]. The actual message is encrypted by a symmetric cipher with a temporary session key. This key is generated at random, since it is the key of a symmetric cipher it must be transmitted somehow to the recipient. This session key is encrypted with the help of the public key of the recipient, for $n$ recipients $n$ different encrypted versions of this symmetric key are stored in the message. The public key algorithm which is used here was RSA in the first versions, newer versions allow different algorithms but prefer ElGamal. Previous versions used IDEA as the symmetric cipher, newer versions prefer triple-DES.

## 5.2   SSL and TLS

Another popular combination of public and secret key algorithms is used to secure the internet, mainly but not limited to encrypted HTTP: SSL, or its successor TLS. It allows a wide range of algorithms for encryption, authentication, or key exchange and many combinations of these algorithms. The first version of the TLS standard is described in RFC 2246 [32], extensions can be found in RFC 3546 [15]. A detailed description of this protocol suite was written by Rescorla [121].

## 6.  Cryptanalysis Overview

As stated in the beginning of this chapter, cryptanalysis is the general term for methods to overcome cryptographic protections. There are several different ways to achieve this goal, in the following we list some, and more can be found in the book of Schneier [131]:

**ciphertext only attack:**  The most cumbersome attack since in this variant the attacker just knows the output of the cryptosystem (and its inner workings, see the Kerckhoff principle), but does not know the input.

**known plaintext attack:**  In this variant the attacker knows about the input data as well

**chosen plaintext attack:**  and here the attacker can even choose the input data.

and more ...

A cipher is considered susceptible to such an attack when the amount of work required for this attack is less than the amount of work for a brute-force attack. A brute-force attack is to try all possible keys until the attacker hits the right key. Methods for known- or chosen plaintext attacks are differential cryptanalysis or linear cryptanalysis, as well as derivatives such as differential-linear cryptanalysis, impossible differentials, higher-order differentials, or the boomerang attack [168]. An overview about such attacks is given in [146].

Besides the above-mentioned methods there are attacks which are not considered pure cryptanalysis but which should be mentioned none the less. These attacks do not try to attack the cipher directly but look at side effects. These attacks look for example at the power consumption of the device while it performs a cryptographic operation: different CPU instructions need different amounts of power, from the power consumption one can make educated guesses concerning secret keys. Another example is to look at the time needed to perform such operations, e.g. a version optimised for CPU speed needs less time for a multiplication when one of the factors is 0. Yet another variant is to look at the electromagnetic radiation. More intrusive methods are to deliberately create errors, e.g. by the injection of wrong signals into a bus connected to the CPU, or by operating the CPU at a temperature not covered by the specification, in such cases the behaviour of the CPU is observed and compared to its operation under normal conditions, from the difference it is possible to gain knowledge about otherwise secret data.

## 7.    Further Information

Additional information on cryptographic algorithms can be found for example in the books of Schneier [131] or Menezes et al. [96]. Security topics in a more general way are covered by Schneier [132], and Kahn [65] covers historical aspects of the art and the science of cryptology. Online-resources are numerous, Peter Gutmann provides an extensive collection of links at http://www.cs.auckland.ac.nz/%7Epgut001/links.html.

## Notes

1 http://csrc.nist.gov/encryption/aes/

2 http://csrc.nist.gov/CryptoToolkit/aes/round2/aesfact.html

3 http://csrc.nist.gov/CryptoToolkit/aes/round2/round2.htm

4 see http://www.media-crypt.com/

5 http://www.wisdom.weizmann.ac.il/%7Eitsik/RC4/rc4.html

Chapter 4

# APPLICATION SCENARIOS FOR THE ENCRYPTION OF VISUAL DATA

## 1. Security provided by Infrastructure or Application

Images and videos (often denoted as visual data) are data types which require enormous storage capacity or transmission bandwidth due to the large amount of data involved. In order to provide reasonable execution performance for encrypting such large amounts of data, only symmetric encryption (as opposed to public key cryptography) can be used. As done in most current applications with demand for confidentiality, public key techniques are used for key exchange or signature generation only (such schemes are usually denoted as "hybrid").

There are two ways to provide confidentiality to a storage or transmission application. First, confidentiality is based on mechanisms provided by the underlying computational infrastructure. The advantage is complete transparency, i.e. the user or a specific application does not have to take care about confidentiality. The obvious disadvantage is that confidentiality is provided for all applications, no matter if required or not, and that it is not possible to exploit specific properties of certain applications. To give a concrete example, consider the distributed medical database infrastructure mentioned in the introduction. If the connections among the components are based on TCP/IP internet-connections (which are not confidential by itself of course), confidentiality can be provided by creating a Virtual Private Network (VPN) using IPSec (which extends the IP protocol by adding confidentiality and integrity features). In this case, the entire visual data is encrypted for each transmission which puts a severe load on the encryption system. The second possibility is to provide confidentiality is on the application layer. Here, only applications and services are secured which have a demand for confidentiality. The disadvantage is that each application needs to take care for confidentiality by its own, the advantage is that specific properties of certain applications may be exploited to create more efficient encryption schemes or that encryption is omitted if not required. Selective encryption of visual data takes advantage of the redundancy in visual data which takes place at the application level and is therefore classified into the second category.

## 2.    Full Encryption vs. Selective Encryption

Over the last years a number of different encryption schemes for visual data types have been proposed, since methods to provide confidentiality need to be specifically designed to protect multimedia content and fulfil the security requirements for a particular multimedia application.

The so called naive method - the most secure one - is to take the multimedia bitstream and encrypt this stream with the aid of a cryptographically strong cipher like AES. Here, the encryption is performed after the compression stage and due to the complexity of the involved encryption algorithm, such a scheme inherently adds significant latency which often conflicts with real-time constraints. Since runtime performance is often very critical in video encoding and decoding, more efficient methods have been proposed. Such systems - often denoted as "selective" or "soft" encryption systems - usually trade off runtime performance for security, and are therefore - in terms of security - somewhat weaker than the naive method. Whereas selective encryption (SE) approaches exploit application specific data structures to create more efficient encryption systems (e.g. encryption of I-encoded blocks in MPEG, packet data of selected layers in JPEG 2000) using secure but slow "classical" ciphers, soft encryption systems employ weaker encryption systems (like permutations) to accelerate the processing speed.

Intuitively, SE seems to be a good idea in any case since it is always desirable to reduce the computational demand involved in signal processing applications. However, the security of such schemes is always lower as compared to full encryption. The only reason to accept this drawback are *significant* savings in terms of processing time or power. Therefore, the environment in which SE should be applied needs to be investigated thoroughly in order to decide whether its use is sensible or not.

In the following we discuss a classification of application scenarios for SE of images and videos (see [114, 143] for more details). The first classification criterion is whether the application operates in a lossless or lossy environment. There exist several reasons why a lossy representation may not be acceptable or necessary:

- Due to requirements of the application a loss of image data is not acceptable (e.g., in medical applications because of reasons related to legal aspects and diagnosis accuracy [176]).

- Due to the low processing power of the involved hardware encoding or decoding of visual data is not possible (e.g. mobile clients).

- Due to the high bandwidth available at the communication channel lossy compression is not necessary.

We do not include this criterion into the classification for simplicity (see [143] for the entire classification).

The second classification criterion is whether the data is given as plain image data (i.e. not compressed) or in form of a bitstream resulting from prior compression. In applications where the data is acquired before being further processed the plain image data may be accessed directly after being captured by a digitiser. We denote such applications as "on-line". Examples for this scenario are video conferencing and on-line surveillance. On the other hand, as soon as visual data has been stored or transmitted once it has been compressed in some way. Applications where compressed bitstreams are handled or processed only are denoted "off-line". Examples are video on demand for lossy compression and retrieval of medical images from a database for lossless compression.

In the following, $t$ denotes the time required to perform an operation, $E$ is the encryption function, $SE$ the selective encryption function, $C$ is compression, $P$ is the preprocessing involved in the selective encryption scheme (where $P$ denotes identification and the extraction of relevant features), and $\gg$ means significantly larger. Please note that the processing time $t$ is not equivalent to computational complexity: for example, if compression is performed in hardware and encryption in software, the time required for compression will be considerably lower as for encryption, contrasting to the relation if both operations are performed in software.

## 2.1   Off-line Scenario:

Given the bitstream $B$ resulting from prior compression, the following condition must be fulfilled in order to justify the use of SE instead of full encryption:

$$t(E(B)) \gg t(P) + t(SE(B)) \tag{4.1}$$

Here, $P$ is the identification of relevant features in the compressed bitstream. Depending on the type of bitstream, $t(P)$ may range from negligibly small to a considerably large amount of time. If the bitstream is embedded or is composed of several quality layers, the identification of parts subjected to SE is straightforward $(t(P) = 0)$, the first part of the embedded bitstream or the base layer is encrypted only. In case of a differently structured bitstream it might be necessary to partially decode or at least parse the bitstream to identify the required parts (e.g. DC or large AC coefficients of a JPEG encoded image), thereby causing $t(P)$ to increase linearly with $t(SE(B))$. However, given an embedded bitstream the condition $t(E(B)) \gg t(SE(B))$ and therefore also equation (4.1) may be satisfied easily and SE definitely makes sense.

## 2.2    On-line Scenario:

Given the raw image data $I$, the following condition must be fulfilled in order to justify the use of SE instead of full encryption:

$$t(C(I)) + t(E(C(I))) \gg t(C(I)) + t(P) + t(SE(C(I)))   \qquad (4.2)$$

Again $P$ is the identification of relevant features in the compressed bitstream and the same considerations about its execution time apply here. Even if $t(P) = 0$, equation (4.2) is very hard to satisfy since $t(C(I)) \gg t(E(C(I)))$ holds for most coding schemes and symmetrical ciphers if both schemes are executed in software. Therefore, the difference between $t(E(C(I)))$ and $t(SE(C(I)))$ often does not matter in practice. This effect is even more pronounced for high compression ratios (since the resulting bitstream after compression is already rather small). Consequently, given the raw image data, the decrease in terms of security often does not justify the marginal savings in processing time as achieved by SE in a software based system.

Regarding the analysis given above, it makes a big difference with respect to the usefulness of SE whether the raw image data or a compressed bitstream is given – this fact is usually ignored in the literature which is a shortcoming in many papers on SE. It is important to analyse the concrete application setting in which SE should be used in order to judge its appropriateness. In the following we discuss SE of a JPEG 2000 bitstream in an on-line scenario in detail.

## 2.3    Selective Encryption of a JPEG-2000 Bitstream

For various proposals how JPEG 2000 files or bitstreams may be encrypted efficiently, see section 2.2.2 (chapter 5). When proposing selective encryption against the approach which encrypts all data we have to compare various aspects of the requirements of the encryption algorithm (AES) and the compression algorithm. For both algorithms we take baseline versions[1], performance enhancements are possible in both cases. In the following, we investigate and compare the number of instructions required by AES encryption and JPEG 2000 compression.

AES performs its encryption on blocks of size 128 bits (=16 bytes). We look at the number of operations per one 128-bit block and then multiply that number by the output bitrate of the compression algorithm (in terms of 128-bit blocks) Table 4.1 shows the number of different operations for one block and for the typical target bitrate of 80000 (= compression ratio of 26 for a $512 \cdot 512$ pixel 8 bpp grayscale image). [] denotes an array lookup operation, = is an assignment, and ⌃ & + % are bitwise exclusive or, bitwise and, addition,

| name | [ ] | = | ^ & + % |
|---|---|---|---|
| KeyAddition | 32 | 16 | 16 |
| ShiftRow | 80 | 32 | 32 |
| Substitution | 48 | 16 | |
| MixColumn | 136 | 32 | 144 |
| 128 bit key, 1 block | 2858 | 944 | 1792 |
| 192 bit key, 1 block | 3450 | 1136 | 2176 |
| 256 bit key, 1 block | 4042 | 1328 | 2304 |
| 256 bit key, 80000 bit | 2 526 250 | 830 000 | 1 440 000 |

*Table 4.1.*   Number of basic operations for AES encryption

| image size (length of one side) | $N$ |
|---|---|
| filter size | $n$ |
| 1 line | $N * n$ |
| 1 image (=total) | $2 * N * N * n = 2N^2 n$ (step size = 2, high+lowpass, horizontal+vertical filtering) |
| level 1 decomposition, 1 line | $\frac{N}{2} * n$ |
| level 1 decomposition, total | $2 * \frac{N}{2} * \frac{N}{2} * n = \frac{N^2 n}{2}$ |
| level $i$ decomposition, 1 line | $\frac{N}{2^i} * n$ |
| level $i$ decomposition, total | $2 * \frac{N}{2^i} * \frac{N}{2^i} * n = \frac{2N^2 n}{2^{2i}}$ |

*Table 4.2.*   Magnitude order of operations for wavelet transform

and modulo operation, respectively. Consequently, for a typical application (80000 bits of output data, 256 bit AES-key) we expect 4 796 250 operations for entirely encrypting the bitstream.

The JPEG 2000 algorithm has to perform some distinct steps to achieve the desired result. The first step is to create the pyramidal wavelet decomposition tree by repeated low- and highpass filtering. The next steps are quantisation and arithmetic encoding of the codeblocks with subsequent rate-distortion optimisation. Table 4.2 displays instruction types and instruction numbers for the filtering process, $N$ denotes the side length of the image and $n$ denotes the size of the filter. Table 4.3 gives an example for an image of size $512 \cdot 512$ pixels, 5 decomposition levels, and the 7/9-biorthogonal filter. The number of operations required by the quantisation and coding stages are not considered in the tables 4.2 and 4.3.

| example values | $N = 512$ pixel side length, $n = 8$ |
|---|---|
| 1 operation includes | 1 addition +, 1 multiplication $*$, 2 array lookups [] |
| 1 decomposition | $2N^2n = 4\,194\,304$ operations |
| standard wavelet decomposition | $\sum_{i=1}^{5} \frac{2N^2n}{2^{2(i-1)}} = 5\,586\,944$ operations |

*Table 4.3.* Numbers of instructions for wavelet decompositions

Figure 4.1 shows that the amount of total execution time of non-filtering related operations in JJ2000 sums up to about 28% of the entire execution time. For the filtering routine, one can expect $5\,586\,944$ operations for the 5-level wavelet decomposition, this number has to be multiplied by 4 since each operation consists of an addition, a multiplication and two array lookups. Additionally, at least $\sum_{i=1}^{5} \frac{N^2}{2^{i-1}}$ assignment operations have to be added. This leads to a total of $22\,855\,680$ basic operations for filtering, resulting in a total of approximately $31\,744\,000$ operations for the entire compression pipeline (by adding the according share of operations for the remaining stages).

We see that the number of instructions for encryption is significantly lower. The wavelet filtering part is mainly determined by the input image size, whereas the operation count for the AES part depends on the output bitrate. This means that the number of operations for both parts depends on the size of the input image, but AES operation count additionally decreases when the compression rate increases.

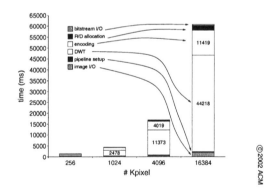

*Figure 4.1.* Runtime analysis of JJ2000 compression for increasing image size

A different aspect is the amount of memory required for data and code and the influence of the memory requirements on the overall execution time. AES requirements are very low, the size of the target data is very small (128 bits), it needs some external lookup tables of small size and the code itself is also very small. Specifically, it fits easily into processor caches which leads to very high execution speeds.

On the other side the requirements of the wavelet filtering part are comparatively high. It has to process the input image, and filter it several times, alternating in horizontal and vertical direction. Typically, such an image has a side length of 256 or 512 pixels. In most cases the filtering step is performed using floating point numbers of double precision (8 bytes). In the 512 pixel case that leads to 2 MB of data. Additionally the algorithm has to access other data, so the input data hardly fits into current processor caches. Options to reduce the memory requirements are the use the integer transform, or to use tiling which unfortunately decreases image quality [95], cache misses are another problem [94].

In our scenario where we compress an input image of size $512 \cdot 512$ pixels (8 bit grayscale) to 80000 bits the calculations above resulted in approximately 31 744 000 operations for JPEG 2000 compression and 4 796 250 operations for AES. So we see that the amount of work performed by the AES part is much smaller than the amount of work of the JPEG 2000 part. In practice, the difference is even higher since the cache effects mainly favour AES. Profiling runs support this assumptions, since the AES part requires below 1% of the total execution time for the full compression/encryption scheme. This means that in the on-line scenario it is reasonable to use full encryption in favour of selective encryption since the savings in terms of computational demand to be expected from SE are marginal (below 1%) and do not at all justify a decrease in terms of security.

Consequently, provided both encryption and compression are executed in software (or both in hardware), applications like video conferencing or surveillance should not employ selective encryption whereas purely retrieval-based applications (e.g. VOD, image database search) can profit significantly from selective encryption.

## 3. Interplay between Compression and Encryption

Note that no matter if lossy or lossless, compression has always to be performed prior to encryption since the statistical properties of encrypted data prevent compression from being applied successfully. Moreover, the reduced amount of data after compression decreases the computational demand of the subsequent encryption stage.

Note also that the involvement of lossy compression technology is usually mandatory in the on-line scenario due to bandwidth restrictions. Consequently, for an on-line imaging application requiring confidentiality during data transfer, the processing chain involves acquisition, compression, encryption, and transmission.

Visual data require a large processing capacity or transmission bandwidth. In case that one or more parties which are involved in an imaging application have strong limits on their processing capacities (e.g. a mobile device with a small battery and a slow processor) or their network link (e.g. a wireless channel), the application needs to be carefully optimised to guarantee minimal energy or bandwidth consumption.

Guaranteeing minimal bandwidth consumption is easy – the image data needs to be compressed to the smallest possible amount of data which often requires high computational effort. In this section we focus on minimal energy consumption in the sense of minimising processing time. Energy minimisation for wireless image transmission has been already discussed in the literature [8, 144]. In [79] it has been found that in the case of the availability of low transmission power it is advantageous to use a less efficient source coder which consumes less power under certain circumstances. In recent work [48], we have discussed the case of confidential transmission of lossless image data and have found that the optimal employment of compression depends on the execution speed of the cryptographic cipher in use. Here, we investigate computationally efficient schemes to provide confidentiality for the transmission of visual data in a lossy on-line scenario. In particular, we seek to optimise the interplay of the three main steps of such a scheme, i.e. lossy compression, encryption, and transmission in the sense of minimal computational effort and energy consumption. Based on exemplary experimental data, we model the costs of the three involved processing steps and subsequently derive cost optimal strategies for employment of confidential visual data transmission in the target environment. Specifically, we aim at answering the question whether JPEG or JPEG 2000 is the optimal lossy compression scheme for this application area.

## 3.1    Basic Building Blocks: Compression, Encryption, and Transmission

The processing chain has a fixed order (compression – encryption – transmission). In the following sections, we introduce the basic technology and model the costs in terms of rate-distortion performance and computational demand of the stages in the processing chain of the target environment.

### 3.1.1    Lossy Compression

JPEG and JPEG 2000 are the most common techniques to compress grayscale or colour images in lossy manner nowadays. They have been already compared with respect to many different aspects [127]. In the context of our work the two interesting aspects are rate-distortion performance and computational demand. It is generally known that the rate-distortion performance of JPEG 2000 is significantly better, especially at low bitrates.

However, this improvement comes at an increased computational cost. The question in the context of our target application is as follows. Given a fixed target quality, does the lower amount of data as produced by JPEG 2000 (which

*Figure 4.2.* Testimages used to evaluate the rate distortion performance.

causes the subsequent encryption and transmission stages to be executed with lower computational demand) justify the higher cost as compared to JPEG? To answer this question, knowledge about the relation of computational costs (i.e. timing behaviour) of the three stages of the processing chain is the key issue.

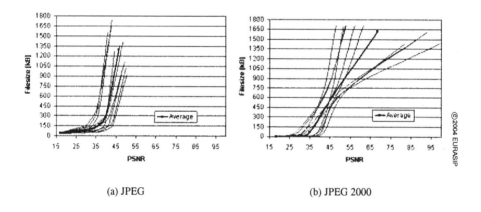

(a) JPEG                    (b) JPEG 2000

*Figure 4.3.* Rate-distortion performance of JPEG and JPEG 2000.

Fig. 4.2 shows the $1780 \times 1308$ pixels 24bpp colour testimages used to rate the compression performance. We use the Jasper JPEG 2000 reference implementation and the IJG JPEG C implementations in order to compress the images to various bitrates. Figs. 4.3 plot PSNR versus filesize for all ten images and show also an average curve obtained by spline approximation.

The better rate distortion performance of JPEG 2000, especially at low bitrates, is clearly confirmed. But also the significant differences in execution speed are confirmed experimentally. On average, Jasper requires 6.12 seconds for compressing an image whereas the IJG implementation suffices with 0.51 seconds on an Intel Pentium III with 1GHz and 256MB SDRAM (this architecture is used for all subsequent measurements as well).

## 3.2    Encryption and Transmission

In order to model encryption behaviour, we use C++ implementations of AES[2] and triple-DES[3]. Fig. 4.4.a plots the size of the data to be encrypted versus the time demand for doing this. It is obvious that triple-DES is much slower as compared to AES. Whereas the amount of difference is partially due to the less efficient implementation of triple-DES, the trend is of course correct in general.

Finally, the transmission stage is modelled by five different transmission media: 56kBit/s modem, 1MBit/s Bluetooth, 10MBit/s ethernet, 11MBit/s IEEE802.11b WLAN, and 100MBit/s ethernet. We use a client-server application which transfers data to the client as soon as the connection has been set up. The client measures the time required to transmit the data after the connection is established.

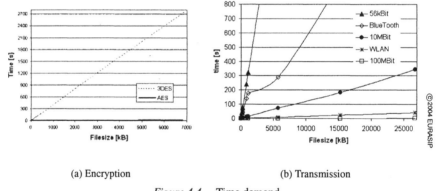

(a) Encryption                                    (b) Transmission

*Figure 4.4.*    Time demand.

In Fig. 4.4.b we plot the size of the data to be transmitted versus the time demand. It is clearly visible that the actual transmission rates are much lower as predicted by the specification. However, the "theoretical" ranking among the different media is maintained in the experiments.

## 3.3    Cost Optimal Configuration of Confidential Visual Data Transmission

The aim of this section is to combine the performance results given in the last section in order to finally answer the question under which "environmental conditions" JPEG or JPEG 2000 might be preferable. This is done as follows. Rate-distortion performance (for fixed sized input images) of JPEG and JPEG 2000 is modelled by two functions $data_i(quality)$, $i = 1, 2$, which require PSNR in decibel (dB) as input and deliver data size in kiloByte (kB) as output (see Fig. 4.3) The input PSNR is the target quality of the transmitted images, $data_i(quality)$ output the resulting file size for JPEG and JPEG 2000, respectively. The average rate-distortion curves as depicted in the figures are used for $data_i(quality)$. Since the aim is to assess the time behaviour of the entire system to identify the least energy consuming setting, we model the overall time function $time(data)$ (input is data size in kByte, output is time in seconds) as the sum of $comptime_i$ (time in seconds required for compression, constant since not dependent on the output bitrate of the codecs), $enctime_j(data)$, $j = 1, 2$ (time required for encryption with AES or triple-DES, input is data size in kByte, output is time in seconds, see Fig. 4.4.a), and $transtime_k(data)$, $k = 1, \ldots, 5$ (time required for transmission over one of the five media considered, input is data size in kByte, output is again time in seconds, see Fig. 4.4.b). Note that spline approximation to measurement data is used for encryption and transmission timings as well. Twenty different functions $time(data)$ are obtained by combining two compression techniques, two encryption modes, and five transmission media.

Finally we obtain functions which output the time demand of the entire processing chain upon input of the desired target quality ($time_l(quality)$) by inserting $data_i(quality)$ into $time(data)$:

$$time_l(quality) = comptime_i + enctime_j(data_i(quality))$$

$$+ transtime_k(data_i(quality)) \text{ for } l = 1, \ldots, 20$$

The spline approximations and the resulting twenty functions $time_m(quality)$ are all generated using MATLAB.

In the following, we always combine the two functions $time_l(quality)$ which correspond to employing JPEG and JPEG 2000 in the same environment (i.e. the same encryption and transmission techniques) into one plot in order to facilitate direct comparison. Fig. 4.5.a shows that in case of AES encryption and Bluetooth transmission the use of JPEG 2000 is faster as JPEG across the entire target quality range. Note that this is also true for all configurations using triple-DES as encryption technique and for all configurations where modem is the transmission medium. In fact, all those plots (which are not shown) actually show the same shape which is very similar to the shape of the rate-distortion curves of JPEG and JPEG 2000. This result corresponds well to the intuitive expectations – if the time demand of encryption plus transmission is very high (as it is of course the case if triple-DES encryption or modem transmission is used), the lower time demand of JPEG as compared to JPEG 2000 is of no relevance for the overall timing behaviour. The final result only reflects the difference in the output bitrate as produced by JPEG and JPEG 2000 and since the timings of encryption and transmission are almost linear in the amount of data, the output bitrate curves are simply linearly upshifted when the functions are combined.

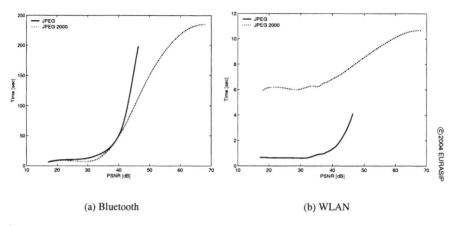

(a) Bluetooth                                    (b) WLAN

*Figure 4.5.*    Wireless connections, AES encryption.

The second wireless link shows a very different behaviour (Fig. 4.5.b). In case of WLAN transmission the use of JPEG is faster as JPEG 2000 across the entire target quality range, and at least five times faster up to 40 dB. This is due to the much higher transmission rate of WLAN as compared to Bluetooth which makes transmission faster and consequently compression speed more and output bitrate less important. Although 10MBit ethernet should deliver almost the same transmission rate as WLAN (11MBit), this is not confirmed experimentally (compare Fig. 4.4). The actual transmission rate is much lower which results as well in a different relation of employing JPEG or JPEG 2000 in the entire processing chain as compared to WLAN. Fig. 4.6.a shows that JPEG is faster as JPEG 2000 only up to 44 dB, below that value JPEG outperforms JPEG 2000 by a factor of 2 at most.

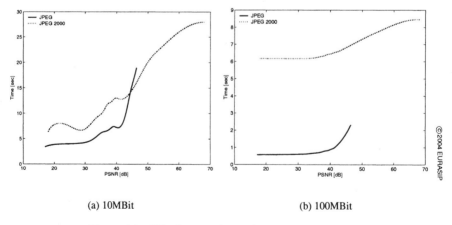

(a) 10MBit                                    (b) 100MBit

*Figure 4.6.*    Wired connections (ethernet), AES encryption

Finally, in the case of 100MBit ethernet, JPEG again outperforms JPEG 2000 across the entire quality range and is more than six times faster up to 40dB. The difference to WLAN is not as pronounced as it would be expected considering the specification of the two transmission modes. This is due to the reduced importance of the contribution of transmission as compared to encryption in case the transmission rate is very high.

Summarising, we have found that in the context of confidential transmission of lossy encoded image data only in case of very slow encryption (triple-DES) and/or slow transmission (modem & Bluetooth) JPEG 2000 outperforms JPEG in terms of overall time demand of the entire processing chain. Only in such environments the data rate reduction of JPEG 2000 as compared to JPEG is significant enough to compensate for the higher time demand of JPEG 2000 compression. It is interesting to note that already in case of AES encryption and WLAN transmission JPEG is significantly faster. In future work we will focus also on GSM and UMTS wireless transmission systems and we will generalise the results for variably sized images.

## Notes

1 The Rijndael AES code was downloaded from
   `http://www.esat.kuleuven.ac.be/~rijmen/rijndael/`, the JJ2000
   JAVA JPEG 2000 reference implementation obtained from
   `http://jj2000.epfl.ch`
2 `http://fp.gladman.plus.com/AES/index.htm`
3 `http://www.ntecs.de/old-hp/s-direktnet/crypt/de/index.html`

# Chapter 5

# IMAGE AND VIDEO ENCRYPTION

Several review papers have been published on image and video encryption providing a more or less complete overview of the techniques proposed so far. Kunkelmann [76] and Qiao and Nahrstedt [120] provide overviews, comparisons, and assessments of classical encryption schemes for visual data with emphasis on MPEG proposed up to 1998. Bhargava et al. [14] review four MPEG encryption algorithms published by the authors themselves in the period 1997 – 1999. More recent surveys are provided by Liu and Eskicioglu [87] (with focus on shortcomings of current schemes and future issues), But [18] (where the suitability of available MPEG-1 ciphers for streaming video is assessed), and Lookabaugh et al. [85] (who focus on a cryptanalysis of MPEG-2 ciphers; in [84] the authors discuss MPEG-2 encryption as an example for selective encryption in consumer applications, the paper having broader scope though). The only monograph existing so far in this area is the PhD-thesis of Kunkelmann [74]. This book covers in-depth discussions and comparisons of MPEG encryption techniques published up to 1998, unfortunately it is written in German.

Image and video encryption are of course closely related by the fact that raw video data consists of a sequence of still images. However, compressed video like the MPEG format is composed of different types of data which can be treated in specific ways by special encryption schemes. As a consequence, we first discuss (still) image encryption techniques in each section which can be applied to still images or single frames (e.g. I-frames in MPEG) in a video. Subsequently, we describe procedures that exploit video specific properties. Additionally, due to reasons explained in the previous section, we distinguish between techniques applied during the compression stage (compression oriented schemes) and techniques applied to an already given bitstream (bitstream oriented schemes).

After describing and discussing the algorithms suggested so far in literature, we provide a final assessment for each technique. For this assessment, we evaluate the following properties:

- **Time demand**: The additional time demand required for the encryption consists of two parts – the time required to perform the actual encryption (denoted as "time(E)") and the time required to identify the parts of the data which are subject to encryption (which may include bitstream parsing or any other preprocessing technique and is denoted as "time(P)"). The time demand is rated as 0, low, medium, high, and may have the additional property of being scalable if depending on the amount of data encrypted.

- **Security**: The security of an entire image and video encryption approach has two aspects. First, the security of the cipher in use itself, and second, the importance and suitability of the data subject to encryption. The security is rated as low, medium, high, and may have the additional property of being scalable if depending on the amount of data encrypted. In accordance to the two aspects of security, two entirely different types of attacks against image and video encryption systems are possible. On the one hand, the cipher in use may be the target of an attack. In this case, common cryptanalytic results about the security of specific ciphers in general apply. On the other hand, in the case of partial or selective encryption, it is possible to reconstruct the visual content without taking care of the encrypted parts. Depending on the importance of the encrypted data for visual perception, the result may range from entirely incomprehensible to just poor or reduced quality. In any case, when conducting such a "direct reconstruction", the high frequency noise originating from the encrypted portions of the data is propagated into the reconstructed frame. In order to avoid this phenomenon, "error-concealment attacks" [174], "perceptual attacks" [85], or "replacement attacks" [104, 106] have been suggested. These types of attacks either try to conceal the quality reduction caused by encryption by treating unbreakable data as lost and then trying to minimise the impact on quality as a result of loss (error-concealment attacks) or simply replace the encrypted parts of the data by either artificial data mimicking simple non-structured content (replacement attacks) or data minimising the perceptual impact of the incorrect data (perceptual attacks).

- **Bitstream compliance**: An image or video encryption scheme is said to be bitstream compliant, if the resulting bitstream is compliant to the bitstream definition of the compression system in use. Bitstream compliance is inherent to any compression oriented encryption scheme if it is based on somehow manipulating coefficient data. On the other hand, bitstream oriented schemes often do not take care about this property at all. Bitstream compliance is rated yes or no.

- **Compressed domain processing**: An important property of image and video encryption schemes is whether they may be applied directly to a given bitstream or the bitstream needs to be decoded before being able to apply encryption. This property is denoted "Bitstream processing" and rated yes or no.

- **Compression performance affected**: As we shall see, quite a lot of image and video encryption schemes increase the file size as compared to applying compression without encryption. This property is denoted as "affecting R/D" (rate-distortion) and is rated yes, moderately, and no.

# 1. DCT-based Techniques

## 1.1 Image Encryption

### 1.1.1 Compression Oriented Schemes

**Zig-zag Permutation Algorithm.** The historically first MPEG encryption proposal is due to Tang [149] and is called "zig-zag permutation algorithm". The idea is to substitute the fixed zig-zag quantised DCT coefficient scan pattern by a random permutation list. Consequently, in the terminology introduced in the previous section this is a soft encryption approach. Additional security measures are proposed as follows:

- The 8 bit DC coefficient is to be split into two 4 bit halves, out of which the MSB part replaces the original DC coefficient and the LSB part replaces the smallest AC coefficient. The reason is that the DC coefficients could be identified immediately by their size thus revealing a low-pass approximation of the image.

- Before DC-splitting, the DC coefficients of eight $8 \times 8$-pixels blocks are concatenated, DES encrypted and written back byte-oriented.

- Instead of using one permutation list a cryptographically strong random bit generator selects one out of two permutation list for each $8 \times 8$-pixels block.

Shin et al. [140] propose a very similar system except that instead of splitting the DC coefficient the sign bits of the DC coefficients are DES encrypted and the DC coefficients are not subject to permutation.

There have been several shortcomings of the zig-zag permutation algorithm identified in literature:

- **Security**

  - Known plaintext and chosen ciphertext attacks: Permutations are known to be vulnerable against known plaintext attacks. Assuming a certain frame of the video is known (the plaintext) – by comparing original and permuted coefficients the permutation list can be retrieved. Even in case two lists have been used the correct one can be found on a per block basis by applying both and using the block with most non-zero coefficients in the upper left corner as decrypted block as shown by Qiao and Nahrstedt [100, 120]. Assuming a decoder is available to an attacker, Uehara and Safavi-Naini [158] also show the analogous weakness against a chosen ciphertext attack.

– Ciphertext only attack: The ciphertext only attack is the weakest attack available to an adversary. In the context of the zig-zag permutation algorithm it is based on the fact that non-zero AC coefficients tend to gather in the upper left corner of the considered image block. Once the non-zero coefficients have been identified in the block, they are shifted to the upper left corner of the block and only a relatively small number of combinations among the non-zero coefficients is required to be tested. Based on some statistical analysis which involves the frequency of non-zero occurrence, Qiao and Nahrstedt give some impressive examples how well images can be approximated using these techniques [120].

- **Decrease of compression performance**: The zig-zag scan as included in the JPEG and MPEG standards orders the coefficients with respect to increasing frequency and decreasing magnitude. As a consequence, long runs of zeros occur in the high frequency areas of a block. The JPEG and MPEG Huffman tables are optimised with respect to those properties – therefore, by changing the zig-zag pattern, some compression performance is expected to be lost. In fact, Qiao and Nahrstedt [120] show a compression performance decrease of up to 45% for MPEG, Zeng and Lei report a bit overhead of 108% for a single I-frame and of 55% for an entire video for H.263 [186], whereas Kailasanathan et al. report decrease up to 20% for JPEG [66].

Shi and Bhargava [138] propose a similar though not equivalent approach. The Huffman codeword list as defined in the MPEG standard is permuted using a secret key, and subsequently used in the compression and decompression process. In order to prevent the algorithm from affecting compression performance only permutations are admissible which maintain the length of the codewords. This limits the number of possible permutations significantly (as already mentioned by the authors) and therefore reduces the available keyspace (and with it the security of the system). Note that contrasting to this approach zig-zag permutation potentially also changes the number of required Huffman codewords (due to different amount and length of zero-coefficient runs) in addition to the resulting permutation of the Huffman table.

| time(E) | time(P) | Security | BS compl. | BS proc. | affects R/D |
|---------|---------|----------|-----------|----------|-------------|
| low | 0 | low | yes | no | yes |

*Table 5.1.* Overall assessment of the Zig-zag Permutation Algorithm

**Frequency-band Coefficient Shuffling.** In order to limit the drop in compression efficiency as seen with zig-zag permutation, Zeng and Lei [185, 186] propose not to permute the coefficients within a single $8 \times 8$ pixels block but to group the coefficients from an entire set of such blocks together and perform permutation to DCT coefficients within a frequency band (i.e. with similar frequency location). This strategy reduces the bit overhead significantly, but still a file size increase of 10 - 20% can be observed [186]. Whereas the security problems as induced by the use of permutations remain valid in principle, the situation is improved as compared to the pure zig-zag permutation approach since additional key material may be employed to define which blocks are used to select coefficients from and the described ciphertext only attack is much more difficult since more blocks are involved.

| time(E) | time(P) | Security | BS compl. | BS proc. | affects R/D |
|---------|---------|----------|-----------|----------|-------------|
| low | low | low | yes | no | moderately |

*Table 5.2.* Overall assessment of Frequency-band Coefficient Shuffling

**Scalable Coefficient Encryption.** Cheng and Li [21] propose to encrypt the low-frequency DCT coefficients only and leave the high-frequency ones unencrypted in the JPEG environment. Their approach is therefore a partial encryption technique. The authors themselves mention that the security of this idea is questionable since when applied to all image blocks edge information remains visible. Kunkelmann and Reinema [77, 76] apply this idea to the MPEG case, use DES or IDEA for encryption, and suggest to use a different amount of coefficients for I and P/B frames. In case the technique is applied to the DCT coefficients, care needs to be taken that the encrypted coefficients exhibit an admissible magnitude to be further processed correctly. In their latter paper Kunkelmann and Reinema apply this idea to the MPEG bitstream instead to coefficients. This of course raises the question of bitstream compliance as discussed in section 1.1.2 (chapter 5) "VLC Codeword Encryption".

Wu and Kuo [177, 178] raise the same security problems with respect to scalable coefficient encryption as Cheng and Li and give visual examples how well edge information can by recovered from material encrypted in the described way. They point out that the concentration of signal energy to a few coefficients as done by most orthogonal transforms does not necessarily imply that the same is true for intelligibility, which is often scattered among all frequency components. Whereas this general observation questions all partial encryption techniques in the DCT domain in principle, wavelet based techniques show different characteristics in this respect.

| time(E) | time(P) | Security | BS compl. | BS proc. | affects R/D |
|---------|---------|----------|-----------|----------|-------------|
| medium+scalable | 0 | low+scalable | yes | yes | no |

*Table 5.3.*  Overall assessment of Scalable Coefficient Encryption (in coefficient domain)

**Coefficient Sign Bit Encryption.**  Zeng and Lei [185, 186] suggest to encrypt the sign bit of each DCT coefficient only (which is a partial encryption approach). The rationale behind this idea is that the sequence of sign bits already exhibits high entropy, consequently, a further increase of entropy caused by encryption (and with it a file size increase after compression) should not be expected. Experimental results involving a H.263 codec even show a small bitrate reduction when applying sign bit encryption. Shin et al. [140] propose to encrypt the DC coefficient sign bit in addition to zig-zag permutation (see above).

Shi and Bhargava [137, 14] propose VEA (Video Encryption Algorithm)) which relies as well on the basic principle to randomly change the sign bits of all DCT coefficients, however, they propose to apply this principle directly on the bitstream (which is possible in principle since coefficient sign bits are separated from the Huffman codewords in the bitstream).

The reduction of computational amount with respect to full encryption is significant since only 13 - 20% of all data need to be encrypted. Encryption of the sign bits can be implemented in many ways: one possibility is to XOR the sign bits with a key stream coming from a cryptographically secure stream cipher, another way would be to apply a block cipher to a set of sign bits where the order of the set equals the block size. However, similar to the case of encrypting a subset of entire DCT coefficients, Wu and Kuo [177, 178] give visual examples of attacked images which have been encrypted using this idea. These examples are fairly impressive which raises severe doubts about the security of this approach.

**Secret Fourier Transform Domain.**  An approach significantly different from those discussed so far is to conceal the transform domain into which the image data is transformed by the compression scheme. The underlying idea is that

| time(E) | time(P) | Security | BS compl. | BS proc. | affects R/D |
|---------|---------|----------|-----------|----------|-------------|
| medium  | medium  | low      | yes       | yes      | no          |

*Table 5.4.*   Overall assessment of Coefficient Sign Bit Encryption

if the transform domain is not known to a hostile attacker, it is not possible to decode the image. Fractional Fourier domains have been used in earlier work to embed watermarks in an unknown domain [37] - Unnikrishnan and Singh [162] suggest to use this technique to encrypt visual data. In particular, the input plane, the encryption plane, and the output plane of the proposed method are fractional Fourier domains related to each other by a fractional Fourier transform. While the security and the size of the corresponding keyspace is discussed (though the latter not in an explicit way), the complexity is not. The authors discuss an optical implementation, but it seems that an implementation on a digital computer would be very costly due to the transforms and the additional encryption involved. It should be noted that no type of compression is involved - the question if this scheme could be somehow integrated into a compression scheme is left untouched. While being an interesting approach in principle, it seems that this technique might be used only in very specific environments and the advantage over a classical full encryption is not obvious.

| time(E) | time(P) | Security | BS compl. | BS proc. | affects R/D |
|---------|---------|----------|-----------|----------|-------------|
| high    | high    | high     | no        | no       | yes         |

*Table 5.5.*   Overall assessment of Secret Fourier Transform Domain

**Secret Entropy Encoding.**   Based on the observation that both, cipher and entropy coder, turn the original data into redundancy-free bitstreams which cannot be decoded without certain information, Wu and Kuo [177] discuss the possibility to turn an entropy coder into a cipher. The information required for decoding is the key in the cryptographic case and the statistical model in the entropy coder case. The authors refer to earlier work where it is shown that is is extremely difficult to decode a Huffman coded bitstream without the knowledge of the Huffman codewords. Shi and Bhargava [138] (see the section on Zig-zag Permutation) suggest a codeword permutation which has a very limited keyspace. Most earlier work on using entropy coders as ciphers has been done for arithmetic coding.

   Wu and Kuo propose to use multiple Huffman coding tables (MHT) out of which a specific one is selected based on random decisions for encoding a given symbol. In order to cope with maintaining the compression ratio, it is suggested to use a different set of training images for each table. Huffman tree mutation can also be used to create a large number of Huffman tables out of 4 initially given tables. In their analysis, the authors state that their approach is vulnerable against the chosen plaintext attack, but not against known plaintext and ciphertext only attacks. In their later work [178], the authors suggest to enhance the security of their scheme by inserting additional bits at random positions and by doing this in different ways for different portions of the data.

| time(E) | time(P) | Security | BS compl. | BS proc. | affects R/D |
|---------|---------|----------|-----------|----------|-------------|
| low | 0 | high | no | no | moderately |

*Table 5.6.* Overall assessment of Secret Entropy Encoding

### 1.1.2 Bitstream Oriented Schemes

**Header Encryption.** The most straightforward to encrypt an image or video bitstream is to encrypt its header. Bitstream compliance is immediately lost and the image or video cannot be displayed any longer using a common player. However, in case an attack is conducted against this kind of encryption, most header informations can simply be guessed or extracted from the syntax of the bitstream itself. As a consequence, the security of such a scheme depends on the type of header data encrypted – if the protected header data can not be guessed or computed by analysing the bitstream, and if this data is crucial for the decoding of the visual data, this approach could be secure. We will discuss this approach for the DCT-video case in some detail in section 1.2.1 (chapter 5) and in section 2.1.4 (chapter 5) for the wavelet case. In any case, header encryption is an interesting approach since it requires minimal encryption effort only.

| time(E) | time(P) | Security | BS compl. | BS proc. | affects R/D |
|---------|---------|----------|-----------|----------|-------------|
| low+scalable | low | low+scalable | no | yes | no |

*Table 5.7.* Overall assessment of Header Encryption

**Permutations.** Permutations are a class of cryptographic systems well suited for designing soft encryption schemes and have been as well proposed to be applied at the bitstream level, however, all these schemes are extremely vulnerable against a known plaintext attack as described in the context of the Zig-Zag Permutation Algorithm. The entities subject to permutation (*basic shuffling units [174]*) are different when comparing the suggestions made so far.

1 **Bytes** Qiao and Nahrstedt [120] discuss the *Pure Permutation Algorithm* where single bytes of an MPEG video stream are permuted. Depending on the security requirements the permutation lists in use can be made longer or shorter. Whereas this approach is extremely fast in terms of the actual encryption process and in terms of parsing the bitstream to identify the data subject to encryption, the semantics of the MPEG stream are entirely destroyed and no bitstream compliance is obtained.

2 **VLC codewords** Based on their earlier Frequency-band Coefficient Shuffling idea [185], Wen et al. [174] and Zeng et al. [184] propose to shuffle VLC run-level codewords corresponding to single non-zero DCT coefficients. Codewords from different $8 \times 8$ pixels blocks are grouped together according to their codeword index and permuted with one permutation list. The number of groups and the range of codeword indices within one group can be adjusted according to security requirements. A problem with this approach is that different $8 \times 8$ pixels blocks usually contain a different number of non-zero coefficients which can be resolved by controlling the "last field" of each block. Format compliance may be guaranteed by truncating codewords eventually exceeding 64 coefficient per $8 \times 8$ pixels blocks, but there is of course significant processing overhead as compared to the Pure Permutation Algorithm induced by identifying VLC codewords and grouping of codewords. Kankanhalli and Guan [67] independently propose exactly the same idea, they further increase the security of their system by additionally flipping the last bit of the codewords randomly and apply corrections if the prefix of the subsequent codeword is affected.

3 **Blocks and Macroblocks** In the same papers, the authors also discuss the use of $8 \times 8$ pixels blocks and macroblocks as the basic shuffling units. Whereas in the case of macroblocks format compliance is guaranteed, in the case of $8 \times 8$ pixels blocks care must be taken about the different VLC tables used to encode inter and intra coded blocks, i.e. these blocks need to be permuted separately or the corresponding flag in the bitstream needs to be adjusted if the type of block was changed by permutation. Obviously, bitstream compliance may be achieved easily using this approach and the processing overhead is also significantly smaller as compared to the codeword permutation case. However, there is an important security problem inherent to this method. This approach is equal to a permutation of (smaller or larger) image blocks in the spatial domain and it is widely accepted that such a technique is vulnerable to a ciphertext only attack. It is only neces-

sary to group blocks with corresponding or similar boundaries together to get a good approximation of the frame.

| Bytes | | | | | |
|---|---|---|---|---|---|
| time(E) | time(P) | Security | BS compl. | BS proc. | affects R/D |
| low | 0 | low | no | yes | no |
| VLC Codewords | | | | | |
| time(E) | time(P) | Security | BS compl. | BS proc. | affects R/D |
| low | medium | low | yes | yes | no |
| Blocks and Marcoblocks | | | | | |
| time(E) | time(P) | Security | BS compl. | BS proc. | affects R/D |
| low | low | low | yes | yes | no |

*Table 5.8.*  Overall assessment of Permutations applied at the bitstream level

To cope with the problem of the known plaintext attack vulnerability of permutations in general, the permutations used for encryption need to be changed frequently. This adds significant load in the area of key management and key distribution which is particularly bad since these operations often involve public-key cryptography. In order to avoid such problems, Wen, Zeng, et al. [174, 184] propose an on the fly generation of permutation lists using parts of the bitstream which are not involved in the permutations (e.g., in case of VLC codeword permutation DES encrypted DCT sign bits could be used, which are not required to be permuted due to their high "natural" entropy). In the following a corresponding example is given [174, 184]:

- Encrypt DCT sign bits (key $K_F$).

- Generate a random bitsequence $R_L$ of length $L$ (using a stream cipher controlled by key $K_L$), with $L > bitlength \times K$ for all $bitlength \times K$, where $K$ is the number of codewords in a codeword table and $bitlength$ is approximately $log_2(K)$.

- For each set of codewords to be permuted, concatenate the encrypted sign bits to $R'$.

- $R'$ is encrypted using $K_F$ which results in the output $R$, which is repeated $bitlength$ times to result in $Rr$.

- $Rc = R_L \ XOR \ Rr$.

- $Rc$ is partitioned into $K$ non-overlapping segments with each $bitlength$ bits. The permutation table maps each index input value $i$ ($0 \le i \le K - 1$) to the $i$-th segment of $Rc$.

Note that the techniques of Wen et al. [174] have been adopted by the MPEG-4 IPMP standard.

Tosun and Feng [157] discuss interesting properties of permutations in the context of wireless video transmission. It is shown that permutations can be the basis of *error preserving video encryption* algorithms in the sense that after a transmission error the incorrect information is not propagated to other parts of the data as it would be the case in classical encryption schemes (caused by the avalanche effect). This is of course desirable in wireless video transmission where large amounts of channel errors occur. Limiting the error after decryption to the location where the error occurred during transmission reduces the task of error concealment considerably as compared to the case where e.g. an entire 128 bit block is destroyed (as it would be the case with AES).

**One-time pad VEA.** Qiao and Nahrstedt [119, 120] propose another partial encryption VEA (Video Encryption Algorithm)) which operates on MPEG streams at the byte level. Odd-numbered and even-numbered bytes form two new byte streams, the *Odd List* and the *Even List*. These two streams are XORed, subsequently the Even List is encrypted with a strong cipher (DES was suggested at that time). The result of the XOR operation and the encrypted Even List are the resulting cipher text. As a consequence, the DES encrypted half of the byte stream serves as a one-time pad for the other half which makes the system fairly secure, because there exists low correlation between bytes and pairs of bytes in MPEG streams (this is confirmed experimentally [119, 120]). This exploits the fact that both compression and encryption decorrelate the data. In order to further increase the security the following improvements are suggested:

- The fixed odd-even pattern is replaced by two randomly generated byte lists (where this is controlled by a $128 - 256$ bit key).

- Each set of 32 bytes is permuted, 8 different permutation lists are employed which are used in fixed order.

- The generation of the two byte lists is changed for every frame (of a video).

This algorithm exhibits very high security but this is achieved at a relatively high computational cost (as compared to full DES encryption, only 47% of the overall computations are saved). Additionally, operating at the byte level the semantic of the MPEG stream is entirely destroyed, bitstream markers may be emulated, and there exists no bitstream compliance after encryption of course.

Tosun and Feng [156] suggest to apply this idea recursively thereby reducing the necessary amount of encryption by one half in each recursion. The Even List which would be subject to encryption in the original scheme is instead again split into an $Odd_2$ List and an $Even_2$ List which are XORed. Now, the

| time(E) | time(P) | Security | BS compl. | BS proc. | affects R/D |
|:---:|:---:|:---:|:---:|:---:|:---:|
| high | low | high | no | yes | no |

*Table 5.9.*   Overall assessment of One-time pad VEA

Even$_2$ List (one quarter of the original data) can be encrypted and the procedure terminates or it is again split into an Odd$_3$ List and an Even$_3$ List. This strategy of course reduces the encryption effort significantly, but the security is also weaker since the one-time pad is no longer one-time in a strict sense [85]. Bitstream compliance is equally destroyed as in the original scheme.

**Byte-Encryption.**   Griwodz et al. [55, 56] propose to randomly destroy bytes in an MPEG stream for free distribution, while the original bytes at the corresponding positions are transferred in encrypted form to legitimate users. This is actually equivalent to encrypting bytes at random positions. The authors find that encrypting 1% of the data is sufficient to make a video undecodable or at least unwatchable. However, the cryptanalysis given is entirely insufficient. Consider the worst case where only MPEG header data is encrypted by chance using this approach. It is well known that header data may be reconstructed easily provided the encoder in use is known. Additionally, no attack scenario is considered but only the case of playing the protected video in a standard decoder is covered. In order to guarantee a certain level of security, a higher amount of bytes need to be encrypted and care needs to be taken about which bytes are encrypted. Wen et al. [174] describe a more general approach as part of the MPEG-4 IPMP standard, named *Syntax Unaware Runlength-based Selective Encryption* (SURSLE). This algorithm encrypts X bits, the next Y bits are left in plain-text, the next Z bits encrypted again, and so on. In addition to the abovementioned security problems, both approaches partially destroy the MPEG bitstream syntax (which is the main security approach of these schemes) and potentially emulate important MPEG markers causing a decoder to crash (which is again desired).

| time(E) | time(P) | Security | BS compl. | BS proc. | affects R/D |
|:---:|:---:|:---:|:---:|:---:|:---:|
| medium+scalable | low | low+scalable | no | yes | no |

*Table 5.10.*   Overall assessment of Byte Encryption

Alattar et al. [6] consider a somehow related approach by encrypting only every other basic encryption unit as opposed to other techniques where all such units are protected, although this is done in the context of a inter-frame encryption approach.

**VLC Codeword Encryption.** Whereas Byte Encryption does not take the syntax of the video into account, VLC codeword encryption does. Contrasting to the permutation of such codewords, strong encryption should be applied in this case. In case bitstream compliance after encryption is not the aim, Byte Encryption applied to a significant fraction of the bitstream is a better choice since VLC codewords need not be identified and therefore bitstream parsing may be avoided to a large extent. In case bitstream compliance after encryption is the aim, when encrypting VLC codewords we face the problem the the encryption of a concatenation of VLC codewords leads not necessarily to a concatenation of valid codewords. For example, given the codewords 0, 10, 110, 111, and a possible concatenation 010, a possible encryption of 010 may lead to 001 which is no valid codeword concatenation and would therefore destroy bitstream compliance. Wen et al. [173, 174] propose a solution to this problem, which has also been adopted for the MPEG-4 IPMP standard. The technique works as follows for a VLC table with $N = 2^k$ entries. Before encryption, a fixed length $k$ bit index I is assigned to each codeword in the VLC table. After a concatenation of VLC codewords is obtained which should be encrypted, a bit string S is constructed by concatenating the indices I of the corresponding codewords. S is encrypted with a secure cipher which results in S'. S' is than mapped back to codewords using the same index-to-codewords map used before for constructing S. The result will be a different concatenation of valid VLC codewords, which are inserted back into the bitstream at the positions of the original codewords. Non power-of-two VLC tables can be treated by decomposing them into several power-of-two tables. While this scheme guarantees a standard compliant bitstream it does not preserve the size of the bitstream. In general, the original and "encrypted" concatenation of codewords will not have the same size (although the number of codewords is equal) – the examples in [174] exhibited an overhead of about 9% of the original filesize. Of course, the computational overhead to identify codewords, build the index lists, perform the mappings, and to reinsert the data is significant.

| time(E) | time(P) | Security | BS compl. | BS proc. | affects R/D |
|---|---|---|---|---|---|
| medium+scalable | high | medium+scalable | yes | yes | moderately |

*Table 5.11.* Overall assessment of VLC Codeword encryption

## 1.2     Video Encryption

Video encryption based on DCT methods is focused on standardised formats like MPEG-1,2,4 or H.26X, therefore all these techniques try to take advantage of the corresponding data formats and bitstreams. Whereas all the techniques discussed subsequently could as well be applied during the compression stage, they are mostly discussed in the context of directly manipulating the bitstream data (after compression has taken place).

### 1.2.1     Bitstream Oriented Schemes

Most schemes for video encryption combine various ideas and are neither purely frame-based nor purely motion-based. Therefore, we will first discuss the main ideas and their properties, subsequently we will describe some complete proposals as given in literature. Note that all techniques described in the section on image encryption may be applied to single frames or the bitstream of videos as well.

**Header Encryption.**     As the second-lowest security level in their SECMPEG scheme (see below), Meyer and Gadegast [97] propose to encrypt all (MPEG) header data of the MPEG sequence layer, group of picture layer, picture layer, and slice layer. Lookabaugh et al. [85] discuss in detail which types of header data are interesting candidates for being encrypted. The data suggested by Meyer and Gadegast to be selectively encrypted turns out to be hardly suited for that purpose (except for the `quantizer_scale_code` field in the slice header). They suggest to encrypt the `macroblock_type` field in the macroblock header since this data covers only about 3.5% of the entire bitstream and its encryption poses severe challenges to a decoder since this field specifies how the following bits are to be parsed and it is a VLC field which may cause the decoder to get out of sync with the bitstream in case it is not correct. Wen et al. [174] investigate the encryption of the *Dquant* parameter (difference of quantisation step size QP between current and previous macroblock), which is a very simple approach since many macroblocks simply use the default settings which makes this parameter easy to attack.

For an overall assessment, see section 1.1.2 (chapter 5).

**Encryption of I-Frames.**     Spanos and Maples [145] and Li et al. [83] independently propose to encrypt I-frames only in 1995. Since P and B-frames are reconstructed based on predictions obtained from I-frames, the main assumption is that if these are encrypted, P and B-frames are expected to be protected as well. This very simple idea has still been suggested in 2003 for a combined DVD watermarking-encryption scheme by Simitopoulos et al. [141] and for a wireless multimedia home network by Taesombut et al. [148]. There are several problems associated with this approach. First, the percentage of the bitstream which is comprised of encoded I-frames is about 25-50% which means that this approach does not reduce the computational complexity to a satisfying extent. Second, the motion in the video remains visible, especially when replacing the encrypted I-frames by uniform frames. A strategy to cope with this would be to increase the number of I-frames which is on the one hand good for security, on the other hand degrades compression performance. For example, increasing the share of I-frames from 1/3 to 1/6 in the "Miss America" and "Flowers" sequences raises the video file size by 50% [4]. Third, and even more severe, the I-blocks contained in P and B-frames resulting from poor prediction results even deliver texture information of I-frames when collected over several frames. This especially affects high motion sequences since in this case P and B-frames contain many I-blocks. Agi and Gong [4] noted this problem in 1996 and suggested to encrypt also these I-blocks. This technique is found as well in one mode of the SECMPEG scheme, in one mode of the combined watermarking encryption scheme of Wu and Wu [179], and has been also suggested in 1999 by Alattar and Al-Regib [5], apparently unaware of all the previous work in this direction. While the security as compared to pure I-frame encryption is increased, the amount of data to be encrypted increases as well (up to 40 - 80%) and the problem of still visible motion content remains unresolved. Additionally, the bitstream parsing effort to identify all I-blocks in P and B-frames is significant. In order to reduce to computational overhead, Alattar et al. [6] suggest to encrypt every other I-block (reducing the encryption percentage to 20 - 40% which is still a lot), however, still the entire approach remains quite insecure.

| time(E) | time(P) | Security | BS compl. | BS proc. | affects R/D |
|---------|---------|----------|-----------|----------|-------------|
| medium  | medium  | low      | yes       | yes      | no          |

*Table 5.12.* Overall assessment of I-frame Encryption

**Encryption of Motion Vectors.** Motion vectors comprise about 10% of the entire data of an MPEG video [85], therefore, restricting the encryption to motion vectors might be an interesting idea. However, from a security viewpoint encryption motion vectors alone can never be sufficient since all texture information from I-frames remains in plain text. Consequently, a video with very low temporal rate would be in plaintext in any case. I-frame material needs to be secured additionally to provide reasonable security. Similar to the DCT coefficient case, motion vector sign bits or VLC codewords can be protected. Some examples are provided in the more comprehensive schemes described below.

| time(E) | time(P) | Security | BS compl. | BS proc. | affects R/D |
|---------|---------|----------|-----------|----------|-------------|
| low     | medium  | low      | yes       | yes      | no          |

*Table 5.13.* Overall assessment of Motion Vector Encryption

**SECMPEG.** SECMPEG defines a new bitstream including a header structure which makes it incompatible with respect to common MPEG players. Besides its data integrity and authentication functionality (which we do not discuss here), five levels of security are defined:

1 No encryption.

2 Header data from the sequence layer down to the slice layer is encrypted.

3 Encrypt same data as in level 2 and the low frequency DCT coefficients of all blocks in I-frames.

4 Encrypt all I-blocks (also those in P and B-frames).

5 Encrypt the entire video.

As can be seen, three different basis techniques are combined into SECM-PEG and all their properties and restrictions apply correspondingly: Header encryption, I-frame encryption, and Scalable Coefficient encryption.

Alattar et al. [6] propose as well a scheme with scalable complexity and security using three levels:

1 Encrypt all data associated with every n-th I-macroblock.

2 Encrypt all data associated with every n-th I-macroblock and all header data of every n-th P and B-encoded macroblocks.

3 Encrypt all data associated with every n-th I-macroblock and all header data of P and B-encoded macroblocks.

Again, Header encryption and I-frame encryption is combined. As a third example for an explicitly scalable scheme we describe the security levels of the combined watermarking encryption scheme by Wu and Wu [179]:

1 Encrypt the DC coefficient of the luminance component of all I frames.

2 Encrypt the luminance and chrominance DC coefficients of all I frames.

3 Encrypt all luminance and chrominance coefficients of all I frames.

4 Encrypt the DC coefficient of the luminance component of all I macroblocks.

5 Encrypt the luminance and chrominance DC coefficients of all I macroblocks.

6 Encrypt all luminance and chrominance coefficients of all I macroblocks.

7 Encrypt the data of all frames (but no header data).

Contrasting to the other two suggestions no header data is encrypted which enables the scheme in principle to deliver compliant bitstreams. Additionally, an explicit distinction between luminance and colour component is made, where securing the luminance component is of course more important from a perceptual viewpoint. The scheme by Wu and Wu again combines I-frame encryption and Scalable Coefficient encryption.

**MVEA and RVEA.** Shi and Bhargava [14, 139, 136] suggest to improve their former algorithm VEA by encrypting the sign bits of the motion vectors in addition to the sign bits of the DC coefficient of I-blocks. This technique is denoted MVEA (if sign bits are randomly changed by a secret key – which is vulnerable to a plaintext attack) or RVEA (if sign bits are encrypted by DES or IDEA). Both, DC coefficients and motion vectors are differentially encoded which causes significant impact when the corresponding sign bits are changed. The authors state that by encrypting motion vector data the content of P or B-frames does not have to be protected further in principle. The give a fixed scan order through the data of a macroblock, at most 64 sign bits are encrypted per macroblock. For I-macroblocks, first the luminance and chrominance DC coefficient sign bits are encrypted, subsequently the lowest frequency AC coefficient sign bits and so on. For P and B-macroblocks, the first sign bits to be encrypted are the sign bits of motion vector data, then the scan proceeds as in the case of I-macroblocks. About 10% of the entire video data consists of sign bit data which makes the approach interesting from the less computations viewpoint.

MVEA and RVEA combine Coefficient Sign bit encryption, Scalable Coefficient encryption, and Motion Vector encryption.

**Techniques in MPEG-4 IPMP.** In their simulations under the MPEG-4 IPMP framework Wen et al. [174] investigate three different configurations with increasing security:

1 Encrypt the FLC coded DCT sign bit, the parameter DQUANT (two bits determining the difference between the quantisation parameter used for the previous macroblock and the current one), and the I-macroblock DC value.

2 Encrypt the VLC motion vector field.

3 Encrypt the data of both previous suggestions.

This proposal combines several techniques as well: I-frame encryption, Co-efficient Sign Bit encryption, Header encryption, Motion vector encryption, and Scalable Coefficient encryption. Whereas the first two options are said to be useful for entertainment purposes only, the third configuration provides satisfying results. However, the authors discuss error concealment attacks against some of the proposed parameters: setting DQUANT and the motion vector field simply to zero, and the DC coefficients to a constant value significantly improves the reconstruction of an encrypted video. The authors therefore propose to combine their suggested encryption configurations with permutations to achieve a higher security level.

## 1.3    Our Implementations of selective MPEG-encryption

### 1.3.1    General Information

For our assessment on the effects of the various encryption method proposed in the literature we recreated a number of them, following their description to a higher or lesser degree. We integrated these encryption schemes into an open-source MPEG encoder called mpeg2enc from the mjpegtools package available at http://sourceforge.net/projects/mjpgtools/. This enables us to compare them in the same environment with the same sequences and settings, like the target bitrate. These experiments may be performed online at http://www.ganesh.org/book/. We conducted our experiments at 4 different target bitrates (800, 1250, 2500, 5000 kbps (kilo Bits per second)), and we used 5 different sequences (Bowing, Surf Side, Coast Guard, Akiyo, Calendar). Sample frames of these images are shown in the appendix on page 139. Although we performed our experiments with all 5 sequences we do not intend to show results from the surf side sequence since there are two major differences with the other sequences which make it hardly comparable: the sequence is very short, and it is no colour sequence.

### 1.3.2    VLC Table Codeword Permutation

The coefficients in a transformed 8*8 DCT block are scanned in zig-zag-order, each non-zero value is encoded using a predefined entry in a VLC (variable length code) table. The actual value does not only depend on this non-zero value, but also on the number of coefficients with 0 value immediately before this value. The entries in this table can be as long as 16 bits, and to be decodable any codeword must not be the prefix of another codeword (this requirement is also called "Fano condition").

A possible way to encrypt a bitstream is to exchange the entries in the VLC table. When a value/runlength pair is encoded a different codeword is retrieved from the table than it would be in the unencrypted case. Several consequences follow: when random codewords are used they are in general not prefix-free.

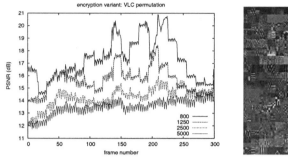
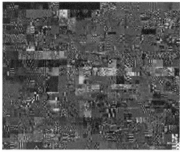

(a) resulting quality for 4 different bitrates          (b) frame #180, bitrate 5000 kb/s

*Figure 5.1.* VLC encryption results with test sequence #1

So the easiest way to generate another set of valid codewords is to use the existing ones and to permute them. In this scenario the encryption key is the seed value for a PRNG which generates to permutation. This approach also gives to opportunity to produce a standard-compliant bitstream. The next problem is that the codewords have been chosen to be as good as possible with respect to compression performance, that means that for combinations which are very likely to appear short codewords are assigned to. An unrestricted permutation disturbs this order and the resulting bitstream is longer than necessary. The countermeasure to this problem is to restrict the permutation further: Just codewords of the same length are allowed to be exchanged. On the other hand this leads to a decreased security: The number of short codewords is limited, but they are very probable. An attacker can expect a high number of them and he can try all possible combinations of them to reconstruct the image, and he can ignore the longer ones. This results in a image lacking the high frequencies. This method is related to the "Zigzag permutation algorithm" on page 47, "Secret Entropy Coding" on page 51, and "VLC Codeword permutation" on page 53.

**Experiments.** This encryption scheme is similar to the VLC codeword permutation described in section 1.1.2 (chapter 5). As you can see in figure 5.1(a) the quality of the resulting encrypted bitstream is below 20dB PSNR in general, with an average of 15dB. In figure 5.1(b) you can see one of the "best" frames, nothing recognisable is left. We can also determine a slight dependence of the quality of the resulting video on the target bitrate.

### 1.3.3    Macroblock Permutation

Each frame within a video consists of the same number of macroblocks, each macroblock contains such data as quantised coefficients from the Y, U and V bands, or motion vectors. A variant to encrypt videos is to exchange the macroblocks within a frame. The key for this encryption method is used as a seed value for a PRNG which generates a permutation.

This is an encryption variant which is annoying but not very secure. The reason is that based on the correlation of border pixels the originally neighbouring macroblocks can be regained. This effect becomes even easier when there are more frames available which are permuted using the same order. So to keep this approach reasonably secure it is necessary to change the key as often as possible, at best with every frame. However the initial insecurity still exists. This variant the variant described in the next section are similar to "Blocks and macroblocks" on page 53.

**Experiments.**    Because the basic shuffling unit here is the macroblock it can be expected that although the entire visual information is present the content can not by recognised instantly. The frames are degraded because the information is not on the expected place. Sequence 3 shows better results than the other sequences (compare figures 5.2(a) and 5.2(c)). This can be easily explained because when a block containing water is exchanged with another block containing water the difference is not very significant (see figure 5.2(b)). Other sequences show "worse" results, e.g. sequence 5 (see figures 5.2(c) and 5.2(d)). The spikes shown on the graphs indicate the I-framesI-frame, the two frames shown were coded as I-frame. When looking at the results of MB permutation encryption we are unable to make out any significant dependency of the resulting quality on the target bitrate, therefore the decision to show the sample frames for bitrate 1250 was random.

### 1.3.4    DCT Block Permutation

Similar to the approach where complete macroblocks are exchanged it is possible to exchange the individual 8*8 DCT coefficient blocks. By permuting the smaller blocks the confusion being created is bigger, and reconstruction becomes more difficult but not impossible. Additionally the algorithm does not discriminate between DCT blocks from the Y plane and DCT blocks from the U and V planes. Again examples with the "best" results (=high PSNR) are shown, in this case sequence 4, see figure 5.3.

**Experiments.**    Figure 5.3(a) shows that the compression rate does not influence the performance of the encryption. Although the image looks indecipherable the same reconstruction method can be applied as in the macroblock permutation method shown above: blocks which are neighbours in the origi-

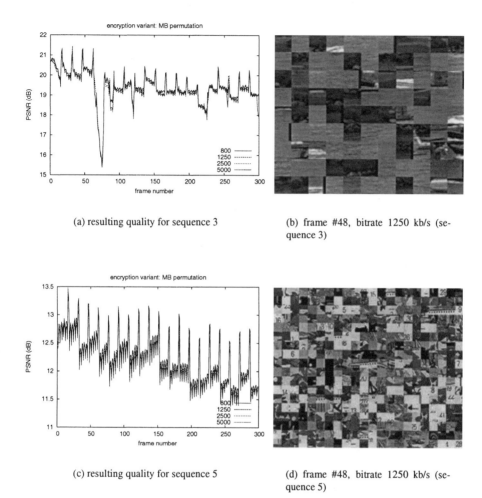

(a) resulting quality for sequence 3

(b) frame #48, bitrate 1250 kb/s (sequence 3)

(c) resulting quality for sequence 5

(d) frame #48, bitrate 1250 kb/s (sequence 5)

*Figure 5.2.* MB permutation, results with test sequences #3 and #5

nal frame have similar pixels at their boundaries, using this correlation many blocks can be recovered. More correlations (respectively a scale factor of 2) exist between the blocks of the U and V plane and the Y plane blocks. The reason that the figure 5.3(b) looks almost random is because some of the 8*8 pixel Y plane blocks end up as 16*16 pixel U or V plane blocks, and vice versa. Therefore a human eye can hardly detect any features.

### 1.3.5 Motion Vector Permutation

Similar to the macroblock permutation and the DCT block permutation it is possible to permute the motion vectors which are assigned to distinctive

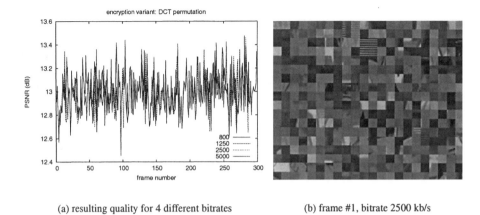

(a) resulting quality for 4 different bitrates          (b) frame #1, bitrate 2500 kb/s

*Figure 5.3.*   DCT block permutation, results with test sequence #4

macroblocks. Within a predicted frame each macroblock can be either an I-block or a predictive block, motion vectors are just assigned to the latter. These vectors can be permuted according to an order provided by a PRNG, where the seed is the key.

The distortion which results from this encryption method is very light, since it affects no I-frames and no I-blocks, and since in many cases many motion vectors within a frame share the same overall direction. However the effects increase with the number of successive P- or B-frames, and they vanish with the next I-frame (obviously). This variant is related to the MVEA and RVEA methods.

**Experiments.**   In this experiment we exchanged the motion vectors. Obviously this method leaves I-blocks and I-frames unaltered. Since the motion vectors are just exchanged within the current frame, but not encrypted or altered otherwise, a global motion (such as a camera pan movement) leads to very small distortions — even when exchanged all motion vectors point to the same general direction. This effect can be partially observed at test sequence #3 (coast guard).

Viewers of such an encrypted bitstream still know about what is going on since they see the keyframes and the visually sensible degradation of the first and last predicted frames is less than in the middle of a GOP (group of pictures). So it is annoying for viewers but not unobservable. Figure 5.4(a) shows the PSNR plot of the encrypted Bowing sequence, during phases with no apparent motion the quality of both I-frames and B/P-frames is approximately the same, but when there is significant motion then the quality drops at the B- and

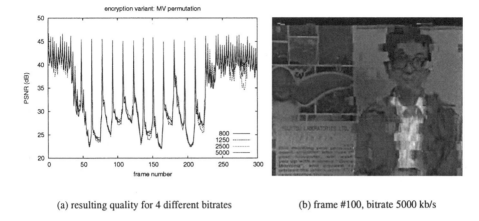

(a) resulting quality for 4 different bitrates　　　　(b) frame #100, bitrate 5000 kb/s

*Figure 5.4.*　Motion vector permutation, results with test sequence #1

P-frames. Figure 5.4(b) is an example for a predicted frame with a medium amount of motion, the PSNR is 27.2dB, the minimum, average and maximum values are 22.2, 33.3 and 46.7 dB, respectively. This behaviour is the reason why this technique has been suggested to be used as a transparent encryption technique (compare section 4 (chapter 5)).

### 1.3.6　Motion Vector Sign Change

Motion vectors are signed values, and therefore another possibility for light encryption is to change to sign bits of these vectors. The actual motion vectors are not stored in the bitstream, they are predicted based upon previous motion vectors, and just the prediction error (residual) is stored. So we have two variants for sign encryption: change the signs of the prediction, and change the signs of the residual.

Again the decision which signs are changed and which are left as they were is based on the output from a PRNG, again with the key as its seed value. And again the distortion generated by this encryption method is very light. A countermeasure is even easier as an attacker has just to try all $2^2$ (in directions $x$ and $y$) or $2^4$ ($x + y$ again, and two fields in the interlaced case) sign combination of either the predicted motion vectors or on the residuals, and then choose the best one — based on the correlation with the neighbour blocks.

**Experiments.**　The encryption of the sign bits is done with the help of a pseudo-random sequence of bits. The algorithm works similar to the encryption method explained above, the permutation of motion vectors. Therefore the effects are similar: I-blocks are unaffected, small amounts of motion cause

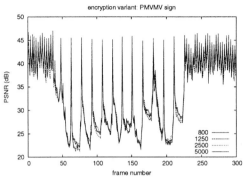

(a) resulting quality for 4 different bitrates          (b) frame #100, bitrate 5000 kb/s

*Figure 5.5.*    Motion vector prediction sign change, sequence #1

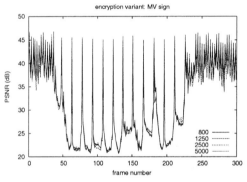

(a) resulting quality for 4 different bitrates          (b) frame #100, bitrate 5000 kb/s

*Figure 5.6.*    Motion vector residual sign change, sequence #1

minor distortions,. . . The quality figures show that the second variant, the encryption of the actually stored/transmitted sign of the residual results in slightly higher distortions (compare figures 5.5(a) and 5.6(a)).

### 1.3.7    DCT Coefficient Sign Bit Encryption

Apart from the motion vectors the transform coefficients are signed values as well. So it is possible to change their signs in a pseudo-random manner as well. There are several variation possible: the most simple variation is to change the sign bits of all blocks. Other variations are to change just the sign bits of I-

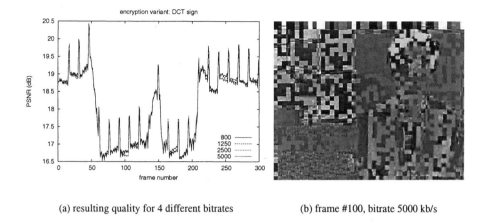

(a) resulting quality for 4 different bitrates          (b) frame #100, bitrate 5000 kb/s

*Figure 5.7.* DCT coefficient sign change, results with test sequence #1

blocks, either just the I-blocks which are located in I-frames, or additionally the I-blocks in predicted frames. The latter can be seen as a complementary option to the various motion vector encryption methods, as they do not change any I-block. For more information see page 50.

**Experiments.** We performed three different experiments as described above: in the first test we allowed to change the sign bits of all DCT blocks. A result can be DCT block seen in figure 5.7, this time the example frame is one of the frames resulting in a low PSNR value. The visual impression is that the colours and the luminance are changed, but it is still possible to get an idea about the contents. This is because the absolute values of the coefficients do not change, this means that blocks with a large amount of high frequency are still blocks with a large amount of high frequency, and blocks with a small high frequency amount are as flat as before: the objects are distorted, but the areas containing edges are recognisable. It is possible, too, that in almost-static scenes which cover more than one GOP averaging might cancel out the strongest effects.

In the other two experiments shown in figures 5.8 and 5.9 the signs of the coefficients of I-blocks were changed in a pseudo-random manner. The difference is that in figure 5.8 I-blocks which are embedded in P- or B-blocks were not encrypted. This makes a significant difference when there is a large amount of motion in the frame, so that the MPEG encoder decides it is better to include I-blocks than residual blocks. In figures 5.8(a) and 5.9(a) we see that the overall performance difference is not very large, just at frames with large motion (the person enters or leaves the view, or bows) the second half of

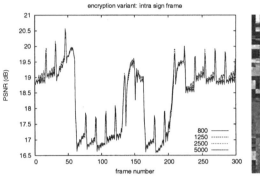

(a) resulting quality for 4 different bitrates        (b) frame #55, bitrate 5000 kb/s

*Figure 5.8.*    I-frame DCT block sign change, results with test sequence #1

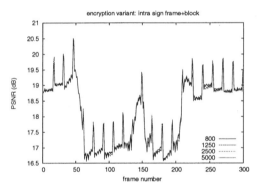

(a) resulting quality for 4 different bitrates        (b) frame #55, bitrate 5000 kb/s

*Figure 5.9.*    I-frame + I-block DCT block sign change, results with test sequence #1

the figures show slightly lower PSNR. The visual difference between figures 5.8(b) and 5.9(b) is obvious: in the second case everything looks "encrypted" whereas in the first case the person in motion can be clearly viewed.

### 1.3.8    DCT Coefficient Mangling

Before the transformed values in an 8*8 block are encoded it is possible to modify them. Individual bits are XOR-encoded with PRNG values. This is prone to generate longer bitstreams since some significant bits which were originally 0 are now changed to 1. To minimise this effect our approach is first

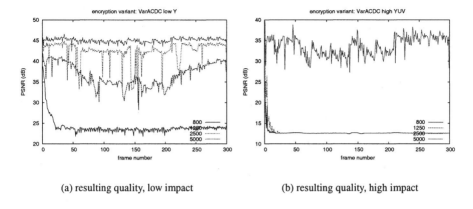

(a) resulting quality, low impact          (b) resulting quality, high impact

*Figure 5.10.* DC and AC coefficient mangling, low vs. high impact, sequence #1

to change just values which are non-zero anyway and second to change just some less significant bits of these values, so that they change just within their order of magnitude.

As it is not known beforehand which values are 0 and which are not, which of these non-zero positions contain large numbers and which do not, one must come up with a predefined scheme which is likely to match these requirements. On the other hand we know that in the low-frequency parts of the DCT block the probability is high to find such values. So we use the following algorithm: Take each of the first $n$ coefficients in zig-zag order, and XOR the lowest $m$ bits with a PRNG value. This can happen for both the Y blocks as well as for the U and V blocks. Carefully choosing $n$ and $m$ allows for a fine-grained tuning of the amount of encryption. This method is related to "Scalable Coefficient Encryption" as shown on page 49.

**Experiments.** The current implementation allows to change bits defined by the same bitmask of the first $n$ coefficients. Usually the bitmask is set to values like 1,3,7 to allow the lowest 1,2,3 bits to be changed. A more flexible approach would change more bits at the first, the DC coefficient, and less and less bits with increasing number of the AC coefficients. A third parameter determines whether to change only some coefficients of blocks in the Y-plane, or additionally the coefficients in the U- and V-planes. With these 3 parameters it is possible to control the degree of the remaining visibility.

We performed the experiments with two sets of parameters. The first set, named "low impact", changes the lowest 2 bits of the first 4 coefficients of the Y-plane. The "high impact" setting changes the lowest 3 bits of the first 8 coefficients of the Y-, U- and V-planes. When we perform these experiments

(a) frame #100, bitrate 5000 kb/s          (b) frame #100, bitrate 2500 kb/s

(c) frame #100, bitrate 1250 kb/s          (d) frame #100, bitrate 800 kb/s

*Figure 5.11.*    DC and AC coefficient mangling with low impact, sequence #1

(a) frame #100, bitrate 5000 kb/s          (b) frame #100, bitrate 2500 kb/s

*Figure 5.12.*    DC and AC coefficient mangling with high impact, sequence #1

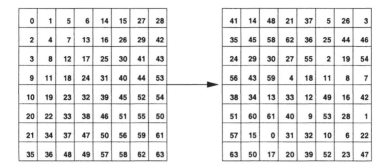

*Figure 5.13.* Modified Scan Order (example)

with varying compression rates we see a strong dependence between the effects of the encryption, the amount of changed bits, and the compression rate. With a high compression rate (i.e. a low bitrate) the effect of changed few bits is better observable than with a low compression rate. With an increasing number of affected bits the effects can be observed on longer bitstreams as well. So we see that it is important to tune the impact of this encryption scheme after the compression rate has been set.

Another experiment is shown on the cover-page of this book. Starting with the upper left image and advancing in scan-line order we encrypt an increasing number of coefficients while we keep the number of affected bits constant: 1,3,6,10,21 coefficients with the 4 least significant bits. When we start at the lower right image and continue left and upwards the number of affected coefficients is constant (15), but the number of affected coefficient bits increases, 1 at the lower right image, then 2,3,4. We meet at the centre with an image which originally was merged from the images of the two authors (see appendix), and then of 21 coefficients the 4 least significant bits were scrambled.

### 1.3.9 Zigzag Order Permutation

After the quantisation in a 8*8 DCT coefficient block the coefficients are encoded together with runs of zeros. The order starts with the DC coefficient, continues with the low frequency AC coefficients and ends with the highest frequency coefficient, the order is a zig-zag curve in the 8*8 block. A method to encrypt the data is to use a different order to encode the data, an example is shown in figure 5.13. Based on a seed for a PRNG the coefficients are permuted before the zig-zag scan is performed. The drawback of this approach is that with the perturbation of the coefficients the natural order does not exist any more, generating uncommon patterns of zeros. This means that VLC codewords with a higher length must be issued, this leads to a lower compression ratio. See also section 1.1.1 (chapter 5).

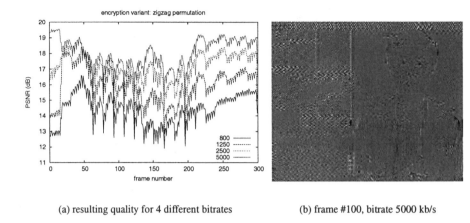

(a) resulting quality for 4 different bitrates          (b) frame #100, bitrate 5000 kb/s

*Figure 5.14.*    Zig-zag order change, sequence #1

**Experiments.**    When the order how the coefficients are coded is changed the effect is that a decoder which is unaware of this encryption sees high-frequency coefficients at a much higher rate than usual. Usually the coefficients are clustered near the DC coefficient, but after this zigzag permutation they are spread out evenly across the whole 8*8 block. The effects can be seen in figure 5.14(b): much high frequency elements, and just a very basic outline of the real frame contents. Since this method affects all block types the differences within a sequence are negligible, and the effects (grey high frequency noise) always similar.

## 1.4    Encryption of Scalable or Embedded Bitstreams

Several techniques described so far clearly show that selectively encrypting visual data implies a significant processing overhead especially when bitstream compliance has to be maintained. In case a selective encryption process requires a multimedia bitstream to be parsed in order to identify the parts to be subjected to encryption, the problem of high processing overhead occurs in general. For example, in order to selectively protect DC and large AC coefficients of a JPEG image (as suggested by some authors), the file needs to be parsed for the EOB symbols 0x00 to identify the start of a new $8 \times 8$ pixels block (with two exceptions: if 0xFF is followed by 0x00, 0x00 is used as a stuffbit and has to be ignored and if AC63 (the last AC-Coefficient) not equals 0 there will be no 0x00 and the AC coefficients have to be counted). Under such circumstances, selective encryption will not help to reduce the processing demands of the entire application [114].

A possible solution to this problem is to use the visual data in the form of scalable bitstreams. In such bitstreams the data is already organised in layers according to its visual importance and the bitstreams do not have to be parsed to identify the parts that should be protected by the encryption process. However, this approach can only be taken if the data has not already been compressed into a non-scalable format (or an expensive format conversion involving partial decompression and scalable recompression needs to be applied). Additionally, the question of rate-distortion performance of the underlying scalable compression schemes is crucial since a higher bitrate of the scalable bitstream would again imply a higher overall encryption effort.

The basic idea of all these schemes is to create a base layer (which contains a low quality version of the visual data) and one or more enhancement layers (which contain the data required to upgrade the quality of the base layer). In an embedded bitstream the first part simply corresponds to the base layer and subsequent parts of the bitstream may be used to create enhancement layers. In this setting, base layer encryption is an interesting and efficient way to provide confidentiality to visual data. Encrypting the enhancement layers on the other hand is called "transparent encryption" (which is discussed in detail in section 4 (chapter 5)) and serves a different purpose, for example it may be used in a "try and buy" scenario.

The MPEG-2 and MPEG-4 scalability profiles provide three types of scalability:

- SNR Scalability: the base layer contains a full resolution but strongly quantised version of the video, the enhancement layers consist of DCT coefficient differences to weaker quantised versions of the data.

- Resolution Scalability: the base layer is a low resolution version of the video (usually generated by repeated weighted averaging and subsequent downsampling), the enhancement layers contain the difference between different resolutions of the data.

- Temporal Scalability: the base layer is a version of the video with reduced frame rate, the enhancement layers simply contain the frames required to achieve higher frame rates.

Additionally, a way has been defined in the context of ATM networks and DVB to partition MPEG-2 data into more and less important parts in order to enable unequal error protection functionality, where leading DCT coefficients and motion vector data constitute the important part and high frequency DCT coefficients the less important part. However, special MPEG units supporting this functionality are required.

In order to overcome the limitations with respect to the small number of possible enhancement layers in those schemes, the MPEG,MPEG-4 FGS (fine granular scalability) mode has been defined. After the creation of a base layer and a single enhancement layer, the latter is encoded in a bitplane oriented mode thereby creating a potentially high number of layers.

MPEG scalability profiles have not found wide acceptance due to several reasons, reduced coding efficiency in case of using a high number of enhancement layers and higher encoding complexity among them. The obvious advantages in the context of confidential video transmission might change this in the future. Additionally, the MPEG committee has recently launched a call for proposals for a scalable video codec which should overcome the problems of MPEG-2 and MPEG-4.

Kunkelmann [74] claims the MPEG-2 data partitioning scheme to be best suited for a base layer encryption approach without giving empirical evidence. Kunkelmann and Horn [76] compare the results of a base layer encryption scheme applied to a spatial domain pyramid vector quantisation codec to a non scalable MPEG-1 partial encryption technique and find it to be superior from the compression and security viewpoint. Tosun and Feng [155] define three layers in an MPEG video which consist of DC and low frequency AC coefficients (base layer), middle frequency AC coefficients (middle layer), and high frequency AC coefficients (enhancement layer). The number of coefficients in these respective layers may be altered adaptively, encryption is applied to base and middle layers only. Only the base layer is guaranteed to be transmitted. In subsequent work [156] the authors focus on wireless transmission and additionally apply forward error correction and an iterative generalisation of the VEA one time pad algorithm which reduces the amount of encrypted data significantly. Eskicioglu and Delp [41] suggest to use Shamirs (t,n)-threshold scheme for a secret sharing based key management scheme in the context of multicasting encrypted multiple layers of scalable video, Eskicioglu et al. [43] provide simulation results for that approach. Yuan et al. [183] propose an encryption scheme for MPEG-4 FGS which encrypts the base layer and the sign bits of the DCT coefficients in the enhancement layer.

While the papers discussed so far focus more on the aspect of reducing the amount of preprocessing for selective encryption by the use of scalable bitstreams, another group of papers focuses onto the networking and streaming aspect. In particular, when streaming visual data over networks with varying bandwidth, bitrate reduction might need to be performed at the network nodes where the networks changes its bandwidth. This poses two problems:

- Encryption/decryption load: In a setting using a conventional bitstream which requires transcoding for rate adaptation, encrypted visual data needs to be decrypted, transcoded, and re-encrypted again. It is evident that this puts severe computational load onto the network node.

- Key management: Even more severe, in order to be able to perform the abovementioned operations, the network node must get access to the key material required for the encryption and decryption process. This implies a significant key management challenge since this might affect several network nodes along the transmission path.

Encrypting scalable bitstreams helps to solve this problem since rate adaptation can be facilitated without the need to decrypt the data – bitrate can simply be reduced by dropping enhancement layer data no matter if encrypted or not. Of course, header data needs to be present in unencrypted form to indicate the regions of a bitstream where enhancement data is located.

Venkatramani et al. [163] describe a very general system architecture where secure adaptive streaming is supported no matter if the underlying data is in scalable format or not. The headers are left unencrypted and in case of non-scalable material several resolutions or quality levels are provided as separate bitstreams which are selected by a streaming server according to the clients' properties. Wee and Apostopoulos [171, 170] introduce a concept denoted as "secure scalable streaming" which provides the abovementioned properties based on scalable compression schemes, network packetisation techniques, and "progressive encryption techniques". The latter are encryption algorithms which match nicely to scalable codecs by allowing encrypted streams to be truncated and decrypted without sacrificing security, like block ciphers in CBC mode or stream ciphers. Based on information stored in the non-encrypted header data, even rate-distortion optimal transcoding may be achieved in encrypted form. Among several wavelet-based codecs, MPEG-4 FGS is discussed as one possible scalable codec to be employed in the system.

### 1.4.1 Experimental Comparison of Layered Encryption Techniques for DCT-coded Data

In this section we systematically compare the different possibilities how to organise DCT-coded visual data into several quality layers with respect to their applicability to selective encryption (compare also [46]). These experiments may be performed online at http://www.ganesh.org/book/.

Since no MPEG software is publicly available which implements all scalability modes, we use the progressive JPEG modes from the JPEG extended system [110]. As we shall see, the different progressive JPEG modes perfectly simulate the types of MPEG scalability. In JPEG, the terminology is changed from layers to scans.

- Hierarchical progressive mode (HP): an image pyramid is constructed by repeated weighted averaging and downsampling. The lowest resolution approximation is stored as JPEG (i.e. the first scan), reconstructed, bilinearly upsampled, and the difference to the next resolution level is computed and stored as JPEG with different quantisation strategy (similar to P and B frames in MPEG). This is repeated until the top level of the pyramid is reached. This mode corresponds well to MPEG-2 resolution scalability.

- Sequential progressive modes

    - Spectral selection (SS): the first scan contains the DC coefficients from each block of the image, subsequent scans may consist of a varying number of AC coefficients, always taking an equal number from each block. This mode is very similar to the abovementioned DVB/MPEG-2 data partitioning scheme.

    - Successive approximation (SA): the most significant bits of all coefficients are organised in the first scan, the second scan contains the next bit corresponding to the binary representation of the coefficients, and so on. Since quantisation is highly related to reducing the bit depth of coefficients, this mode behaves similarly to SNR scalability.

The JPEG standard also allows to mix different modes – an important example is to use the DC coefficient as first scan, the subsequent scans contain the binary representation of the AC coefficients as defined by successive approximation (we denote this mode as mixed (MM)). The three modes allow a different amount of scans. Whereas spectral selection offers a maximum of 64 scans, the hierarchical progressive mode is restricted to 5 or 6 sensible scans (given a $2^8 \times 2^8$ pixels image). Successive approximation mostly uses a maximum of 10 scans (depending on the data type used for coefficient representation). Similar to the scalability profile of MPEG-2, the JPEG progressive modes are not used very much and are poorly supported and documented in commercial software. Although providing much better functionality for transmission based applications, the compression performance could be expected to decrease using JPEG progressive modes. As a matter of fact, compression performance is at least as good as for the baseline system and often better (Fig. 5.15 shows the rate distortion performance of the Photoshop baseline and progressive JPEG versions). However, the computational demand for encoding and decoding is of course higher.

This also serves as an excellent example how poorly documented the progressive JPEG modes are – there is no hint in the Photoshop documentation what type of progressive mode is employed. All subsequently used images are in 8bpp $512^2$ pixels format.

As discussed before, the basic idea of selectively encrypting visual data in layered representation for providing confidentiality is to simply encrypt the base layer or the scans containing the perceptually most relevant information. In this case, the enhancement layers or remaining scans may be expected to contain data which is useless on its own although given in plaintext. Of course, this is not true in case of temporal scalability since the enhancement layer contains entire frames. As a consequence, temporal scalability can not be used for layered encryption.

Decoding a partially en-crypted image by treating the encrypted data as being unencrypted leads to images severely degraded be noise type patterns (which originate form the encrypted parts, see Figs. 5.16.a and 5.17.a). Using these images to judge the security of the system leads to misin-terpretations since a hostile attacker can do much better. In particular, an attacker could

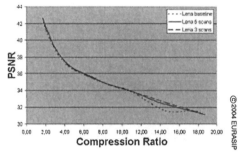

*Figure 5.15.* Compression performance (Lena image with $512^2$ pixels and 8bpp) of Photoshops' base-line JPEG and progressive JPEG (with 3 and 5 scans).

simply ignore the encrypted parts (which can be easily identified by statistical means) or replace them by typical non-noisy data. This kind of attack is called "error-concealment" [174] or "replacement attack" [112] in the literature.

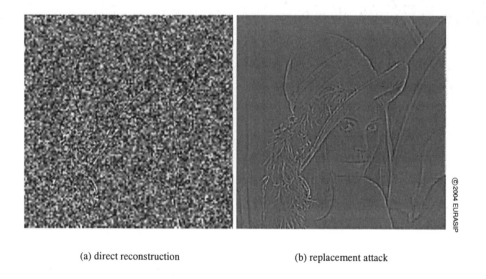

(a) direct reconstruction      (b) replacement attack

*Figure 5.16.* Lena image; a three level pyramid in HP mode is used with the lowest resolution encrypted

Figs. 5.16.b and 5.17.b clearly show that there can be still information left in the unencrypted parts of the data after selective encryption has been applied – in case of direct reconstruction this is hidden by the high frequency noise pattern. As a consequence, in order to facilitate a sound evaluation and comparison of the four modes to be considered, they are evaluated after a replacement attack has been mounted.

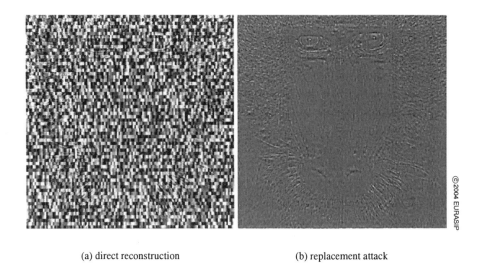

(a) direct reconstruction                           (b) replacement attack

*Figure 5.17.*    Mandrill image; SS mode is used with DC and first AC coefficient encrypted

In order to be able to compare the different JPEG progressive modes for their suitability to follow the selective encryption approach, we set the amount of data to be encrypted to approximately 10 and 30%, respectively. Since we use a 10 bit representation for quantised DCT coefficients, the percentages can be exactly achieved in SA mode by encrypting the corresponding number of bitplanes. For HP, we get 31.25% of the original data encrypted by building a three level pyramid and encrypting the lowest resolution plus the first residual, and 8.3% by building a six level pyramid and encrypting the lowest resolution plus the three next residuals. SS facilitates protection of 29.7% and 9.3% of the data by encrypting 19 or 6 coefficients, respectively. Finally, we achieve encryption of 31.09% and 11.4% in the case of MM by scrambling the DC coefficients and one bitplane or three bitplanes, respectively.

The replacement attack is conducted as follows: for HP, the encrypted first scan is replaced by data originating from an equally sized image with constant gray value and eventually encrypted residuals are replaced by constant zero residuals. For SS an encrypted bitplane is replaced by a constant 0 bitplane, and for SA the encrypted coefficients are replaced by zeros.

Table 5.14 shows the PSNR values of the different techniques applied to the Lena and Mandrill image. Note that in contrast to a compression application, a method exhibiting low PSNR values is most desirable (since this implies low

| | HP | SS | SA | MM |
|---|---|---|---|---|
| Lena, 10% enc. | 14.8 | 14.6 | 7.0 | 6.8 |
| Lena, 30% enc. | 14.7 | 14.5 | 6.2 | 6.4 |
| Mandrill, 10% enc. | 17.5 | 16.8 | 7.5 | 7.3 |
| Mandrill, 30% enc. | 17.0 | 16.2 | 6.4 | 6.4 |

*Table 5.14.* Objective quality (PSNR in dB) of reconstructed images

image quality and therefore good resistance against the replacement attack). HP and SS show very similar results (at about 14.5 - 17.5 dB depending on the image and percentage of encryption) as well as do SA and MM at a much lower level (at 6.4 - 7.5 dB). However, it is interesting to note that there is not much numerical difference between the encryption of 10% and 30% of the data. As a consequence, we expect to perform SA and MM much better in terms of security as compared to HP and SS. In Fig. 5.18 we visually compare the reconstructed images underlying the numerical data of Table 5.14.

The numerical results are clearly confirmed by visual inspection. Whereas HP and SS clearly exhibit still remaining high frequency information (which are much clearer in the HP case), almost no information is visible for SA and MM where the images are dominated by noise. This noise comes from the fact that on average 50% of the coefficients (no matter if high or low frequency) have been altered at their MSB in the binary representation which results in those randomly looking images. Note that the replacement attack is not effective in the case of SA and MM since no matter if directly reconstructed or under the replacement attack always on average 50% of the coefficients are altered at their MSB position. Although the results of SA and MM look rather satisfying from a security point of view, there is still visual information related to the original image left. Fig. 5.19 shows that this remaining information may be enhanced using simple image processing operations which leads to the conclusion that obviously MM is the most secure variant of our investigated selective encryption schemes and is the only one that can be securely operated at a level of encrypting 10% of the data. The additionally encrypted DC coefficient makes MM much more resistant against reconstruction as compared to SA.

Increasing the amount of encrypted data up to 30% does not leave any perceptually relevant information in the remaining data in the case of SA and MM. Little information is left in case of SS applied to the Lena image, HP still reveals some edge and texture information. The Mandrill image contains much high frequency information which is still visible but not recognisable after encrypting 30% for both, the HP and SS modes.

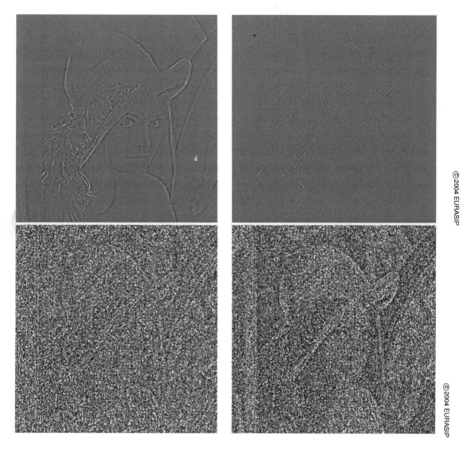

*Figure 5.18.* Subjective quality of reconstructed Lena image, 10% of the data encrypted (HP,SS,SA,MM, in clockwise direction starting at the upper left image).

We have seen that selective encryption using the hierarchical progressive and spectral selection JPEG modes still leaves perceptually relevant information in the remaining data after encrypting 30% of the original image data. Successive approximation and especially a hybrid variant which additionally protects the DC coefficient deliver much better results in terms of security. Relating these results to the MPEG case, SNR scalability will be most suited to apply selective encryption to scalable video data.

## 2.    Wavelet-based Techniques

Wavelet-based techniques devoted to video encryption have not been discussed in literature so far, although all proposals made for image encryption may be applied to each frame of a video independently of course. The lack of a wavelet-based video coding standard explains this situation. As in the section

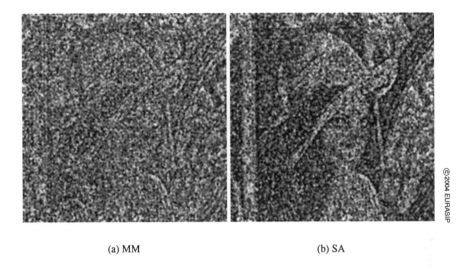

(a) MM                                    (b) SA

*Figure 5.19.*    Images from Fig. 5.18 median filtered (3x3 kernel) and blurred (5x5 filter).

on DCT-based techniques, we distinguish between schemes operating during the compression stage ("compression oriented") and schemes applicable to a given bitstream ("bitstream oriented'). Note that most wavelet-based compression schemes use arithmetic coding as their entropy coding stage which does not provide a one-to-one correspondence among symbols and codewords like Huffman coding as used in DCT-based systems does. Therefore, techniques manipulating single coefficients cannot be employed in the transform domain.

## 2.1    Compression Oriented Schemes

### 2.1.1    Coefficient Selective Bit Encryption

Similar to their proposals for DCT-based systems, Zeng and Lei [185, 186] suggest to encrypt selected parts of the transform coefficients' binary representation. They compare refinement, significance, and sign bits with respect to their entropy and compressibility. Based on this analysis, it is suggested to encrypt bits that are not highly compressible due to their high entropy and low intercorrelation. The corresponding selection limits the influence of the encryption process to rate-distortion performance: sign bits and refinement bits. Of course, refinement bit encryption can be used only as an additional security technique since it does not provide enough confidentiality as a standalone approach. Similar doubts with respect to security of sign bit encryption are valid as in the DCT case. Corresponding experimental results are provided by Zeng and Lei who propose to combine sign bit encryption in combination with other techniques like block permutation or block rotation (see section 2.1.3 (chapter 5)).

| time(E) | time(P) | Security | BS compl. | BS proc. | affects R/D |
|---------|---------|----------|-----------|----------|-------------|
| medium | medium | low | yes | no | no |

*Table 5.15.* Overall assessment of Coefficient Selective Bit Encryption

### 2.1.2 Coefficient Permutation

In the context of DCT-based compression systems, coefficient permutation has been proposed as a means to provide confidentiality within the compression pipeline (compare the "Zig-zag Permutation Algorithm" in section 1.1.1 (chapter 5)). In the context of wavelet-based compression schemes, random permutation lists have been proposed by Uehara et al. as well to secure wavelet-subbands [159]. One obvious advantage as compared to the DCT scenario is that the distribution of wavelet coefficients is image dependent and therefore the vulnerability against ciphertext only attacks does not occur. Also, it is claimed [159] that contrasting to the DCT case the observed drop in compression performance is about 2% only.

In this section we use random permutation lists to secure wavelet-coded visual data (compare also [105]). We show that a system based on randomly permuting wavelet-subbands incorporated in the JPEG 2000 or the SPIHT coder generally delivers much worse results in terms of compression performance as given in [159]. The comparison of JPEG 2000 and SPIHT in this context provides interesting insights with respect to the correctness of the zerotree hypothesis.

**Encryption Using Random Permutation of Wavelet-Subbands.**    The basic approach is to permute the wavelet coefficients of different wavelet subbands with dedicated permutation keys. A permutation key is defined as a vector of length $n$, and $n$ wavelet coefficients can be encrypted using this key. We use an algorithm according to Knuth's "Seminumerical Algorithms" to compute uniformly distributed permutation keys.

In case permutation keys have to be transmitted along with the compressed image data (and not generated on the fly as proposed in [174]) the used keys have to be protected and therefore be encrypted with a standard encryption scheme like AES. For example, the key data itself can be inserted conveniently into the JPEG 2000 bitstream taking advantage of the so-called termination markers.

Encryption based on random permutation lists has been shown to be vulnerable to known plaintext attacks. The use of more different keys increases the overall security of the system. This raises the question how many keys should be used to encrypt the data and what key lengths should be used in order to achieve a satisfying level of security. Additionally it needs to be considered that any key information needs to be stored in the final bitstream and decreases the compression performance. We discuss two key management scenarios:

1  full key scenario: A wavelet subband with $n$ pixels is permuted with a "full" key of length $n$.

2  key for row scenario: A wavelet subband consisting of $n$ pixels $(n = r * c, r = rows, c = columns)$ is permuted with keys on a per row basis. Therefore, a number $x, 1 <= x <= r$ of keys with length equal to one row $c$ is used, and the keys are exchanged in a round robin fashion.

Instead of using randomly chosen permutation keys which need a significant amount of additional storage capacity, a master key together with a key generation algorithm as proposed in [159] can be used to save memory. The usage of a master key with a key generation algorithm can be somewhat weaker in terms of security as compared to using randomly selected keys, however, it turns out that this approach is mandatory to limit the loss in compression efficiency.

**Experimental Results.**    We use the two considered lossy image compression schemes with the default decomposition depth. The testimages are the Lena, lunge, plane, and the graves image each at a resolution of $512 \times 512$ pixels.

Regarding the "key for row" key management scenario we discuss the worst case in terms of security, where the same permutation key is used for each row of a wavelet subband.

In order to evaluate the compression performance, each testimage is encoded with both considered coding algorithms. Within the coding pipeline, the coefficients of the wavelet subbands are permuted before the quantisation stage. Thereafter, the encrypted and compressed file is decoded, the corresponding wavelet-subbands are inverse-permuted, and the overall rate-distortion performance is computed.

The rate-distortion performance for the lena image is shown in figure 5.20. Note that key material is not included in the bitstream for this comparison. The "no permutation" curve denotes the rate-distortion performance of the original JPEG 2000 and SPIHT algorithm. The curve "key for row" shows the performance when all subbands are permuted and per subband only one key is

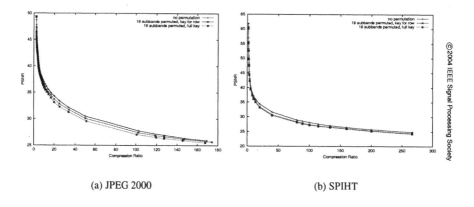

(a) JPEG 2000                                    (b) SPIHT

*Figure 5.20.*   Compression performance, Lena image 512 x 512 pixels

repeatedly used for the rows of the subband, and the curve "full key" shows
the rate-distortion performance, when each subband gets a full key for the permutation of the whole subband.

In the case of JPEG 2000 a max. drop of compression performance of 26%
using full keys can be observed when coding the lena image (meaning that the
encrypted file needs to be increased by 26% in order to achieve the PSNR of
the original encoded image; we denote this to be a loss of compression performance of 26%), and only a 13% decrease can be observed when using one
key for each row of a subband. Table 5.16 lists the observed maximal drops
of compression performance for all tested images. Overall, the "key for row"
method degrades compression performance much less, and the zerotree-based

|                        | full key | key for row |
|------------------------|----------|-------------|
| JPEG 2000, lena512     | 26%      | 13%         |
| JPEG 2000, lunge512    | 8%       | 4%          |
| JPEG 2000, plane512    | 27%      | 14%         |
| JPEG 2000, graves512   | 21%      | 5%          |
| SPIHT, lena512         | 26%      | 21%         |
| SPIHT, lunge512        | 9%       | 9%          |
| SPIHT, plane512        | 23%      | 21%         |
| SPIHT, graves512       | 22%      | 15%         |

*Table 5.16.*   JPEG 2000/SPIHT: all subbands permuted, max. observed file size increase at a
medium compression rate ranging from 25 up to 45

SPIHT algorithm produces similar results in the "full key" scenario as compared to JPEG 2000. The latter is surprising, since permuting the coefficients of wavelet subbands obviously destroys the zerotree structures which should be essential to the performance of such an algorithm. Considering the zerotree hypothesis, a stronger degradation would have been expected in the SPIHT case which raises doubts about the correctness of this important assumption. However, in the "key for row" scenario the JPEG 2000 compression performance is much less decreased as compared to SPIHT. This is due to the spatial correlation which is preserved among pixels in neighbouring areas (since the same permutation is used for adjacent rows), which allows the context-based arithmetic coding engine of JPEG 2000 to produce better results as compared to the inter-subband zerotree coding of the SPIHT codec.

Compared to the good results shown in [159] both considered schemes produce a significant performance loss (up to 27%), and we do not even include the key data in the final compressed file yet. The compression scheme in the referenced work is not a very sophisticated one (first generation wavelet coding scheme) and SPIHT as well as JPEG 2000 depend much more on pixel context as simple scalar quantisation based schemes.

| time(E) | time(P) | Security | BS compl. | BS proc. | affects R/D |
|---------|---------|----------|-----------|----------|-------------|
| low | 0 | medium | yes | no | yes |

*Table 5.17.* Overall assessment of Coefficient Permutation

### 2.1.3 Coefficient Block Permutation and Rotation

Zeng and Lei [185, 186] also propose a generalisation of the coefficient permutation approach. They suggest to divide each subband into a number of blocks of the same size. The size of these blocks can vary from subband to subband. Within each subband, blocks of coefficients are permuted according to a permutation key which should also differ from one subband to another. Since the local statistics of the wavelet coefficients are preserved, the expected impact on coding performance is smaller as compared to the pure coefficient permutation case (the degradation is the smaller, the larger the block size is selected). On the other hand, using large blocks threatens security due to two reasons:

- The permutation key is small.

- A possible attacker might try exploit edge continuity in the high pass subbands and a smoothness constraint (similar to the attacks against line permutation in the spatial domain, see section 3.1.1 (chapter 5)) in the low pass subband to invert the permutation.

To further increase security without affecting rate-distortion performance it is suggested to additionally use one of eight isometries of each block (which corresponds to rotating and flipping the block). This makes it harder to invert the permutations based on image properties, however, a higher number of rotated versions would be necessary to provide sufficient security.

| time(E) | time(P) | Security | BS compl. | BS proc. | affects R/D |
|---------|---------|----------|-----------|----------|-------------|
| low     | 0       | low      | yes       | no       | moderately  |

*Table 5.18.*   Overall assessment of Coefficient Block Permutation and Rotation

### 2.1.4    Secret Transform Domains

Similar to the idea of using a secret Fourier transform domain (compare section 1.1.1 (chapter 5)) it is also possible to use secret wavelet transforms for an encryption application. The idea of using secret wavelet domains has also been used to increase the security of watermarking schemes. In this context, filter parameterisations [34] and wavelet packet subband structures [33] have been used to conceal the embedding domain.

Contrasting to the Fourier case, all proposals concealing the wavelet transform domain for encryption are integrated into a compression pipeline. Vorwerk et al. [166] propose to encrypt the filter choice used for wavelet decomposition, however, this suggestion remains vague and is not supported by any experiments. In the following we discuss two ways of generating a large variety of wavelet filters out of which a secret one may be chosen for actual decomposition. All these techniques have a significant advantage: the amount of data subject to encryption is minimal since only information about the transform in use needs to be encrypted. Therefore, these methods may be seen as a special variant of header encryption. However, two questions remain unanswered so far:

1  Since a vast share of the data remains unencrypted, is it possible to reconstruct the visual data (or at least a good approximation to it) using the unencrypted material ?

2  Filter choice is important with respect to image quality in wavelet compression schemes. Can the compression quality be maintained when using any of these approaches?

**Secret Wavelet Filters: Codebook Approach.**    Generalised wavelet decompositions (where different filters are used at different decomposition levels) may be employed and the structure of these decompositions may be kept as

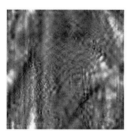  

*Figure 5.21.* Reconstruction using random filters

*Figure 5.22.* Reconstructed image where the heuristic failed at the finest level of decomposition

*Figure 5.23.* Reconstructed image where the heuristic failed at 3 out of 5 levels

key: here non-stationary multiresolution analysis NSMRA [31, 88, 160] or subband variant decompositions (which use the same idea applied for wavelet packet decompositions at the subband level) [161] are possible candidates. We use a library consisting of predefined filters. The size of the keyspace then depends on the size of the filter library ($l$), the decomposition depth ($k$), and the type of generalised decomposition (i.e. $l^k$ keys for NSMRA and $4^{l^k}$ keys for subband variant decomposition).

In the current implementation we chose the NSMRA approach [113], the index of the filter in the library can be chosen by different algorithms.

Figure 5.21 shows the case when random (i.e. wrong) filters are used to reconstruct the image.

Concerning a possible attack against the scheme, we assume the attacker has all knowledge except the indices of the actual filters in use. A brute-force attack is not feasible but by using the following heuristics we get a sufficient result: when the correct filter is applied in the reconstruction process, a rather smooth image results, but when the filter is incorrect, artifacts appear and the resulting image is quite noisy. We measure the difference between neighbouring pixels (both vertical and horizontal) and then we calculate the entropy of these differences. If the filter is correct then the entropy will be low. This heuristic reduces the attack complexity from $l^k$ for brute force to $l \times k$. The heuristics work in most cases, figures 5.22 and 5.23 show reconstructed images where the heuristics fail. These images show that even an partially incorrectly guessing heuristic is better than a pure random attack.

The described attack shows that this scheme is only secure enough for a low-security entertainment application in case the codebook is not very large. The number of different wavelet filters discussed in literature is too small to provide codebooks with sufficient size. In the next section, we will discuss techniques to generate entire families of wavelet filters for that purpose.

| time(E) | time(P) | Security | BS compl. | BS proc. | affects R/D |
|:---:|:---:|:---:|:---:|:---:|:---:|
| low | 0 | low | yes | no | moderately |

*Table 5.19.*  Overall assessment of Secret Wavelet Filters: Codebook Approach

**Secret Wavelet Filters: Parametrisation Approach.**  For the construction of compactly supported orthonormal wavelets, solutions for the dilation equation have to be derived, satisfying two conditions on the coefficients $c_k$ ($\phi(t) = \sum_{k \in \mathbb{Z}} c_k \phi(2t - k)$, with $c_k \in \mathbb{R}$). Here we use parameterised filters generated according to an algorithm proposed by Schneid and Pittner [130]:

Given $N$ parameter values $-\pi \leq \alpha_i < \pi$, $0 \leq i < N$, the following recursion

$$c_0^0 = \frac{1}{\sqrt{2}} \text{ and } c_1^0 = \frac{1}{\sqrt{2}}$$

$$c_k^n = \frac{1}{2}\Big((c_{k-2}^{n-1} + c_k^{n-1}) \cdot (1 + \cos \alpha_{n-1})+$$

$$(c_{2(n+1)-k-1}^{n-1} - c_{2(n+1)-k-3}^{n-1})(-1)^k \sin \alpha_{n-1}\Big)$$

can be used to determine the filter coefficients $c_k^N$, $0 \leq k < 2N + 2$. We set $c_k = 0$ for $k < 0$ and $k \geq 2N + 2$. Example filters which can be generated using this formula are the Daubechies-6 filter, which can be constructed using the parameters $(0.6830127, -0.1830127)$, or the Haar filter which is generated with the parameter 0.

The number $N$ of parameter values $\alpha_i$ controls the length of the resulting wavelet filter, i.e. $2N + 2$.

Note that similar parameterisations are available for biorthogonal filterbanks [59] and for the lifting scheme in the context of JPEG 2000 [134].

In this section we investigate the properties of a header encryption variant where we keep the parameter to generate the filters for the wavelet transform secret (compare also [73]). This can be easily achieved in the context of JPEG 2000 Part II by simply encrypting the corresponding field containing the custom filters in the header using a cryptographically strong cipher. As a consequence, the amount of data subject to encryption is minimal, since no actual image data but only filter coefficients are protected.

In the following, we investigate the compression quality and the security of the resulting scheme, experiments are performed using the JPEG 2000 Jasper C reference implementation with different decomposition filters.

Whereas the traditional filters used for wavelet compression are tuned for optimal concentration of the energy contained in the image and the separation of high- and low-frequency parts, parameterised filters provide a wide quality range. The advantage as well as the disadvantage of parameterised filters is their variety, not all filters within such a family are equally suited for a specific purpose, in this case, image compression. Fig. 5.24 shows the resulting quality (PSNR in dB) when compressing the 8 bpp $512 \times 512$ pixels Lena image using different parameter values with compression ratios 10 and 20, respectively.

It is clearly displayed that the compression quality of the filters resulting from the parameterisation algorithm varies in the interval $[29.5dB, 35dB]$ for ratio 10 and $[25dB, 30dB]$ for ratio 20, respectively. Among other variations, obviously the left half of the parameter range leads to poor filter quality. As a consequence of these findings, a strategy is required to limit the possible compression quality loss in-

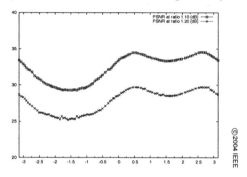

*Figure 5.24.* Quality of JPEG 2000 compression, using a 1-dimensional parameter space

troduced by randomly chosen parameters. The most desirable approach would be a heuristic which – given either the parameters to generate the filters or the actual filter coefficients themselves – could determine an approximation of the compression quality to be expected in advance (i.e. without performing the compression). A heuristic of this type would allow a parameter generation and evaluation on the fly, i.e. during the compression stage without significant increase of computational demand. Besides restricting the parameter to positive values no such heuristic could be found.

To avoid low-quality filters, two other approaches might be possibly used:

■ Generate the parameters and the corresponding filter coefficients and perform the compression stage. The parameter is used only in case the quality turns out to be sufficient. As this technique is time consuming, it contradicts our goals we want to achieve with the entire system. Only one failure in parameter choice (i.e. one bad quality filter) makes the scheme significantly more expensive than full AES encryption of a JPEG 2000 Part I bitstream.

■ Determine parameter values of good quality in advance and restrict the admissible parameters to regions close to that values. Fortunately, the quality of parameters is very much image independent, which makes this approach a feasible and efficient one. However, the decrease of the amount of admissible parameter values is known in advance (also to a potential attacker) and needs to be considered. This fact reduces the overall security of the system since it corresponds to a smaller keyspace.

In the following we focus on the security of the system. The restriction in terms of filter quality values reduces the amount of admissible parameter values as seen before to 20 – 50 % of the entire range, depending on the quality requirements of the target application. At first sight, there seem to be enough parameter values left since the data type of the parameters for this kind of filter is $\mathbb{R}$ (in theory), in practice it is $\mathbb{Q}$. However, close parameters lead to similar filters which in turn lead to similar wavelet transform coefficients. Of course, this might be a threat to the security of the system since an attacker does not need to know the compression parameter exactly to get a "decrypted" image with sufficient quality. In Fig. 5.25 we illustrate this problem. The Lena image is compressed with filters generated by the parameter 1.05841, and subsequently decompressed with a large number of different filters derived from parameters covering the entire possible range. We plot the PSNR of the resulting images against the parameter used for decompression. The desired result would be an isolated single quality peak at the position of the "correct" parameter (that one used for compression) and low values everywhere else.

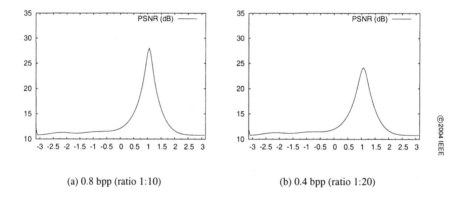

(a) 0.8 bpp (ratio 1:10)                          (b) 0.4 bpp (ratio 1:20)

*Figure 5.25.*    Attack against a 1-D parameter scheme, JPEG 2000 compression at ratios 1:10 and 1:20

The result of this experiment is not an isolated PSNR peak but an entire region centred around the correct parameter where the PSNR values are decreasing with increasing distance from the correct value. For example, the parameter range [0.75, 1.25] (which covers about 8 % of the entire parameter range) provides image quality above 20 dB. Fig. 5.26.a visualises an image decompressed with a parameter displaced from the correct one by a distance of ≈0.2 in terms of parameter value. Obviously, the quality of this (attacked) image is too high to provide any kind of confidentiality.

(a) 21.86 dB, parameter 1.20841          (b) 10.78 dB, parameter 2.85841

*Figure 5.26.*    Quality of attacked images, JPEG 2000 compression at 0.4 bpp

As a consequence, the number of admissible parameter values needs to be restricted to a rather sparse grid. Taken this fact together with the beforementioned restrictions due to low quality filters the keyspace is too small for a reasonable application in case of the 1-D parameter scheme. However, when taking these restrictions into account the quality of encrypted and attacked images is low enough for applications where the size of the keyspace is not an issue (see Fig. 5.26.b).

In order to increase the available keyspace parameterisations with more parameters (leading to longer filters) can be used. This increases the number of high quality filters significantly if the percentage of good filters remains approximately constant in the entire set of filters, which turns out to be true. To compare the 1-D parameterisation to the 2-D case, the Lena image is compressed with the filters generated by the parameters -1.69159 and -1.84159, and subsequently decompressed with a large number of different filters derived from parameters covering the entire possible range. In Fig. 5.27 we again plot the PSNR of the resulting images against the parameter used for decompression.

The result shows that still a sparse grid needs to be applied to this much larger parameter space. In the 2-D parameter scheme we do not result in the single isolated PSNR peak as well but we still face an entire region where the quality of the encrypted and attacked images is too high. Therefore, the resulting number of admissible parameters still remains rather small in the 2-D case, but the strategy to move to higher dimensional parameterisation schemes turns

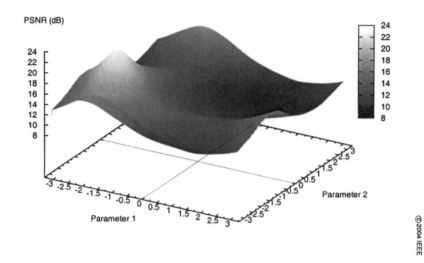

*Figure 5.27.*   Attack against a 2-D parameter scheme, JPEG 2000 compression at ratio 1:10

out to be fruitful in principle and leads to reasonable keyspace sizes at least for low security applications. Fig. 5.28 shows two encrypted and attacked images using the same 2 parameters for compression as given before. The result suggests that a sufficient degree of confidentiality may be achieved with the proposed scheme, provided the limitations as discussed before are addressed properly.

Theoretical and practical work in the field of image and video compression usually prefers biorthogonal filters. In most compression applications the well-known "Biorthogonal 7,9" filter is used. Therefore our hope was that this filter is not an exception but an indication about the superiority of the overall class of biorthogonal filters in this context [164].

For the creation of biorthogonal filters we relied mainly on a paper by Hartenstein [59] because a method was presented which allowed an "easy" implementation: no symbolic computations with programs like *Mathematica* or *Mathlab* were required. Such a prerequisite would have negated the requirement that many tests with different parameters should be performed, and that the program should be able to perform a very quick filter exchange. Additionally, this application should fit into the context of the C++ based compression library and framework developed at our department (called `libganesh++`) which includes the SMAWZ-codec used in the following experiments (compare also [118]). Besides Hartenstein some other authors have proposed addi-

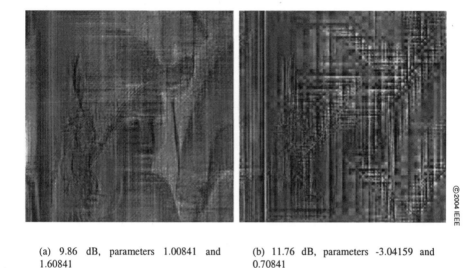

(a) 9.86 dB, parameters 1.00841 and 1.60841

(b) 11.76 dB, parameters -3.04159 and 0.70841

*Figure 5.28.* Quality of attacked images, JPEG 2000 compression at 0.4 bpp

tional methods for parameterising biorthogonal wavelet filters [122, 108, 111, 93, 92, 69, 64, 107].

Even length filters require that the difference between high- and low-pass filter is a multiple of 4, i.e. $4K$. The general formula to generate these filters is

$$\left[ \begin{array}{c} H(z) \\ G(z) \end{array} \right] = H_p(z^2) \left[ \begin{array}{c} 1 \\ z^{-1} \end{array} \right] \tag{5.1}$$

$$\text{with } H_p(z) = A\Lambda(z)S_{L-1}\Lambda(z)\dots\Lambda(z)S_0 \tag{5.2}$$

$$\text{and } \Lambda(z) = \left[ \begin{array}{cc} 1 & 0 \\ 0 & z^{-1} \end{array} \right] \tag{5.3}$$

$$\text{and } S_i = \frac{1}{\cos^2\theta_i - \sin^2\theta_i} \left[ \begin{array}{cc} \cos\theta_i & \sin\theta_i \\ \sin\theta_i & \cos\theta_i \end{array} \right]. \tag{5.4}$$

It is obvious that the denominator above must not be 0, therefore the $\theta_i$ are limited to $\theta_i \neq (2k+1)\frac{\pi}{4}, k \in \mathbb{Z}$. Hartenstein had two errors in his paper, one in his equation (2) where he had an excess matrix $S_L$, and the other one in his equation (3) where the restriction for $\theta_i$ was too strict. Additionally, he didn't care about the energy-preserving property of his matrices: the value of the determinant must be 1. So Hartenstein didn't give the fraction part for the matrices $S_i$. The above limitation for $\theta_i$ has to be extended in practise, so that it can be formulated like "$\theta_i$ should not lie within a neighbourhood of $\epsilon$, centred at odd multiples of $\pi$". The result is undefined right at these multiples, but within the neighbourhoods numerical instabilities occur which make it difficult to calculate reasonable results. We discovered that $\epsilon$ must be increased for increasing absolute values of $K$.

We can distinguish between three cases, for each one a different Matrix $A$ must be constructed:

**$K = 0$:** this is the simplest case

$$A = \frac{1}{\sqrt{2}} \begin{bmatrix} 1 & 1 \\ 1 & -1 \end{bmatrix} \tag{5.5}$$

**$K > 0$:** the high-pass filter is longer than the low-pass filter

$$A = \begin{bmatrix} 1 & 1 \\ P_{0K}(z) & P_{1K}(z) \end{bmatrix} \tag{5.6}$$

(this was equation (5) in the Hartenstein paper)

$$P_{0K} = \begin{cases} 1 & K = 0 \\ 1 + \tan\beta_1 z^{-1} - z^{-2} & K = 1 \\ P_{01}(z^k) + \sum_{j=2}^{K} z^{j-K-1} q_j(z) & K > 1 \end{cases}$$

$$P_{1K} = \begin{cases} -1 & K = 0 \\ 1 - \tan\beta_1 z^{-1} - z^{-2} & K = 1 \\ P_{11}(z^k) + \sum_{j=2}^{K} z^{j-K-1} q_j(z) & K > 1 \end{cases}$$

with $q_j(z) = \tan\beta_j - \tan\beta_j z^{2(1-j)}$.

**$K < 0$:** the low-pass filter is longer, the formula is almost identical (and we set $K = -K$ to be positive):

$$A = \begin{bmatrix} Q_{0K}(z) & Q_{1K}(z) \\ 1 & -1 \end{bmatrix} \tag{5.7}$$

with $Q_{0K}(z) = P_{0K}(z)$ and $Q_{1K}(z) = -P_{1K}(z)$

Of course the matrix A must be normalised again, otherwise the subsequently generated filter will not preserve the energy of the signals.

In the following, we investigate the quality of compression conducted by even-length filters.

The quality obtained by compression using even-length parameterised biorthogonal filters according to the construction method of Hartenstein varies by a very large amount, even more as compared to the orthogonal case. As

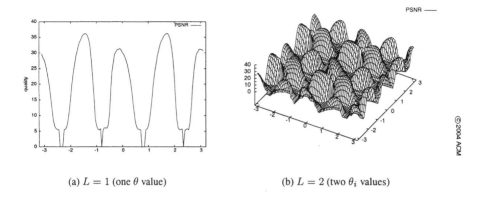

(a) $L = 1$ (one $\theta$ value)          (b) $L = 2$ (two $\theta_i$ values)

*Figure 5.29.* Quality values for $K = 0$.

can be seen on figures 5.29(a) and 5.29(b) the maximum value is near 35dB, but values go down to 5 dB as well. Note that at the instances where the filter could not be generated because of numerical instabilities a quality value of 0 was assumed. Some of the figures shown in this paper were generated from the results with tests with the Lena image, some with the baboon image — there are no significant differences between these two result sets. In all experiments the images were compressed with a target bitrate of 80000 bits, this leads to a compression rate of about 6.5 for 8-bit gray-level images with 256*256 pixels.

First we look at the most simple case where both filters have the same length ($K = 0$). We examine the results with $L = 1$ and $L = 2$. Figure 5.29(a) shows the first case, we observe a very high variance of the PSNR values. Figure 5.29(b) shows the results obtained by setting $L = 2$, the results look very similar to the previous figure. One can also observe some regular pattern with high-quality areas which could be used for later encryption tests.

When we compare the figures 5.30.a and 5.30.b we see a difference in the maximum PSNR of about 10dB: 24.7 versus 34.6 on the other hand. This shows that it is important to make the right choice between a long high-pass filter together with a short low-pass filter or the short high-pass with the long low-pass filter: the variant with the shorter high-pass filter for decomposition is the better choice. Figure 5.31 shows the frequency response for both filters.

Another interesting point is the comparison of the aforementioned filters with the well-known 7/9 filter: the PSNR in the same experiment lies at 37.7dB. Figure 5.31(c) shows the frequency response of the 7/9 filter. In comparison to figures 5.31(a) and 5.31(b) this looks much better: higher degree of symmetry, and the frequency separation into two bands is much higher. On the other hand the symmetry is lower when we compare it with the frequency response

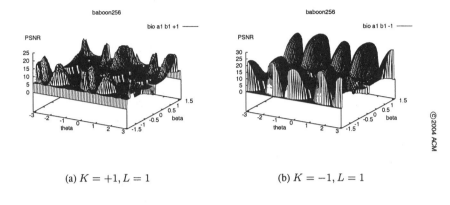

(a) $K = +1, L = 1$                                    (b) $K = -1, L = 1$

*Figure 5.30.*   Parameterised biorthogonal 4/8 filters.

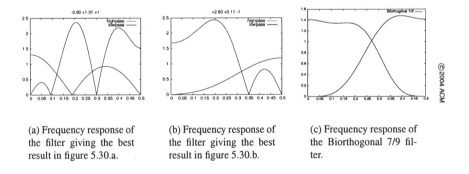

(a) Frequency response of          (b) Frequency response of          (c) Frequency response of
the filter giving the best          the filter giving the best          the Biorthogonal 7/9 fil-
result in figure 5.30.a.            result in figure 5.30.b.            ter.

*Figure 5.31.*   Frequency response

of orthogonal parameterised filters [118], so this attribute can be a hint towards high-quality filters. But it is widely known that there are other parameters important for compression performance, too.

So we see that when one wants to implement parameterised biorthogonal filters for selective encryption one will be faced with a decreased quality when using the same compression rate, at least when applying even-length filters derived from Hartensteins parameterisation.

We see that even length biorthogonal wavelet filters derived from a parameterisation proposed by Hartenstein have turned out to give extremely varying (and also generally poor) compression results thus making them inappropriate for a selective encryption approach which only protects the filters in use during wavelet decomposition and compression.

| time(E) | time(P) | Security | BS compl. | BS proc. | affects R/D |
|---------|---------|----------|-----------|----------|-------------|
| low | 0 | low | yes | no | moderately |

*Table 5.20.* Overall assessment of Secret Wavelet Filters: Parametrisation Approach

**Secret Subband Structures.** In this section we propose to use wavelet packet based compression instead of pyramidal compression schemes in order to provide confidentiality (compare also [113, 115–117]). Header information of a wavelet packet (WP) image coding scheme based either on a uniform quantiser or on zerotrees is protected, in particular we use AES to encrypt the subband structure used by the encoder only. In our approach the encoder uses different decomposition schemes with respect to the wavelet packet subband structure for each image (in fact, the subband tree is chosen randomly or determined by some pseudo-random algorithm). These decomposition trees are encrypted and have to be present at the decoder to be able to reconstruct the image data properly.

In our WP based selective encryption approach we do not use a classical best basis selection or a similar method to determine a useful wavelet packet basis, but we use a more-or-less random decomposition tree. This tree can be generated completely random, or using a PRNG (pseudo random number generator) algorithm to decide the decompositions, it is also possible to use a best-basis algorithm as a first step and make random or pseudo-random alterations to it. Using a decomposition tree generated by the best-basis algorithm without further alterations is not reasonable since such trees share common features for many images which would consequently facilitate an attack.

We use the PRNG approach in this work. In order to decide if a certain subband should be decomposed further, first a number is obtained from the PRNG which generates equally distributed float numbers in the interval $[0, 2[$. A weight is computed at every decomposition level: weight at level $i =$ base value $+ i \cdot$ change factor.

Then the PRNG number is divided by the weight. If the result is smaller than 1, no further decomposition is computed. The reason for introducing the weight is that in case of using PRNG numbers only "shallow" decompositions are more probable than many "deep" decomposition trees. The default values for "base value" and "change factor" are 1 and 0, respectively. The probability that decomposition level $i$ is reached for a given subband is $(\frac{1}{2})^i$ when the default values are used. This means that the probability that the decomposition tree has a depth of exactly one level is $\frac{1}{2}$.

The subband tree carrying the subband structure information of the data is secured (by using AES encryption) for transmission. The amount of data is

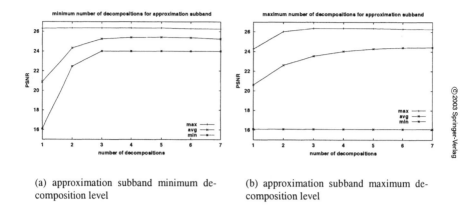

(a) approximation subband minimum decomposition level

(b) approximation subband maximum decomposition level

*Figure 5.32.*   minimum and maximum level of decomposition influencing the quality

very low compared to e.g. an approach which encrypts the tree structure of spatially quadtree decomposed images [22] where up to 50% of the overall data are encrypted. In our approach just the PRNG seed value and the two weight factors have to be secured, otherwise the hierarchy information has to be encrypted, 1 bit per subband, which leads to a typical amount of 50 to 200 bits since the decomposition depth has to be limited.

In contrast to classical WP coding schemes we do not employ subband structures specifically tailored for compression but random ones. Therefore, we need to examine the typical rate-distortion performance of the entire system, i.e. how much quality we possibly lose by using this approach. From these results we derive parameter settings to limit this potential quality loss.

We performed our tests with the image "Lena" and cross-checked the results with a subset of the tests using the image "Barbara", again using the SMAWZ codec operating at 80000 bits. In our tests we varied 6 parameters, as partially shown in figures 5.32 and 5.33. All figures show two or three lines, the maximum PSNR value achieved with a certain parameter combination, the average value and (sometimes) the minimum. Values near 16dB correspond to decompositions where just one decomposition step was performed for the approximation subband (see figure 5.32(a)).

The parameter which has the most influence on the compression quality is the parameter determining the minimum number of decompositions of the approximation subband (see figure 5.32(a)). Setting the minimum number to 2 or lower the probability is high that a decomposition results which gives a bad compression result. Setting the value too high (e.g. 6) can give slightly decreased results as well. In order to limit quality loss, we propose a value of 4 or 5 for this parameter.

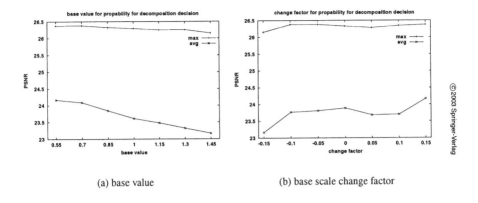

(a) base value                                    (b) base scale change factor

*Figure 5.33.*   Various weight factors for the decomposition decision influence on the quality

The parameter which comes next in terms of determining compression quality is the number of maximum decompositions allowed for the approximation subband as shown in figure 5.32(b). We suggest a value of at least 5 but preferably higher since a high value for this parameter significantly increases the number of admissible subband trees which is important for the security of the system. The latter two parameters are intercorrelated since min $\leq$ max.

The degree of influence of the remaining parameters is low as long as they are set to reasonable values. In particular, the maximum number of decompositions allowed for any subband does not seem to have any impact on compression performance for values $\leq$ 7. Therefore, this parameter should also be set to the highest reasonable value (i.e. 7) to guarantee a potentially high number of subband trees.

In the following, the two factors determining the weight are investigated in more detail. The "base value" gives the initial probability determining the decomposition decision. At a value of 1 the two possibilities are equal, when the number is lower than 1.0 the decision favours further decompositions. As can be seen in figure 5.33(a) in this case the quality is slightly better. We suggest to set this value to 1.0 or below. The "change factor" changes the weight in a decomposition depth dependent way. If the change factor is 0, the "base value" stays the same on all decomposition levels. Otherwise it is added to the "base value" at every level of decomposition thereby increasing the weight at each decomposition level.

Based on intercorrelation results between figures 5.33(a) and 5.33(b) (not shown), we suggest that the "change factor" value is set to 0.0 (in the case when the above "base scale factor" was set to 1.0) or 0.15 (if the "base value" was set to a value smaller than 1.0).

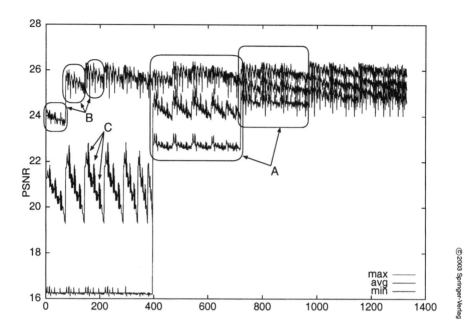

*Figure 5.34.*    All parameters of figures 5.32(a), 5.32(b), 5.33(a), 5.33(b) in one plot

Fig. 5.34 gives an overall impression; it shows a combination of the previous parameters, where every value on the x-axis denotes a fixed parameter set. The variation using the seed values for the PRNG gives 50 values, and from these one maximum, average and minimum are computed.

Clusters of PSNR-values with different magnitudes are evident, and they result from the order used for the loops over the arguments to collect and aggregate the PSNR values. Clusters of the three biggest sizes were labelled "A", "B" and "C" in the figure: Areas marked as "A" denote the "outer loop", each bubble (and the neighbours which are not explicitly marked) contains samples generated with the same value for the parameter "minimum number of decompositions of the approximation subband". Areas like "B" contain samples with a fixed value for "maximum number of decompositions of the approximation subband". Since the maximum number must not be smaller than the minimum and both parameters have a maximum of 7 it is clear that the number of samples with an identical minimum decomposition depth for the approximation becomes smaller with increasing values. This also means that the width of the "A" bubbles decreases. Entries marked with "C" show identical values of the next parameter, in this case our "base value". The remaining factors are almost invisible at this resolution.

As a consequence of these results, we set the minimum number of approximation subband decompositions to 4 and the corresponding maximum value to 7. The maximum number of allowed decompositions for any other subband is set to 7. The "base value" and the "change factor" are set to 0.55 and 0.15, respectively. These settings improve the compression performance of admissible wavelet packet trees significantly: the maximum is 26.19 dB, the minimum is 24.98 dB, and the average of all subband trees is 25.60 dB.

In the following, we focus on possible attacks and their complexity. We assume that the attacker has all knowledge about the coder except the key for the symmetric cipher (AES) which protects the subband tree structure information. To be able to reconstruct the tree the attacker has four possibilities:

1 Break the cipher,

2 Reconstruct the tree with the help of unencrypted data.

3 Exhaustive search for the correct subband structure,

4 a different, yet unknown method

Using AES as symmetric cipher the first option is computationally infeasible. In the following we provide some details concerning the options 2 and 3.

First we discuss the reconstruction of the subband structures if a uniform quantiser is used for coding. We assume that the coefficients are stored in a subband oriented manner, i.e. coefficients of one subband correspond to a contiguous part of the bitstream. Within every single subband the coefficients are stored in scanline order, going from left to right, and each line from top to bottom. The subbands are traversed in depth-first order. If a different scan order for the coefficients would have been used (e.g. scanning the tree structured image data in one run for all values, line by line), then some details in the following procedure had to be changed but the overall method stays the same. In any case, in order to reconstruct the image, the attacker has to superimpose a subband structure.

We demonstrate that this can be done by exploiting the distinct statistical properties of WP subbands in two basic steps: first, reconstruction of the size of the approximation subband and second, reconstruction of the remaining tree

Of course, the most important step in this attack is to reconstruct the size of the approximation subband since here the most important information is concentrated. The statistics for the approximation subband differ significantly from the detail subbands: In the approximation there is roughly an equal distribution of all values, in the detail subbands many values are close to 0, and only few coefficients have high values (positive and negative as well). Because of this difference the separation is achieved fairly easily. We use the following formula to estimate the distribution of the coefficients, a slightly modified variance

$$v = \frac{1}{N-1} \sum_{i=1}^{N} (x_i - m)^2$$

– $m$ is the previously computed average of all coefficients and $N$ denotes the number of coefficients currently examined. This means that we compute the distance of the first $N$ coefficients from the average of all coefficients. $v$ is evaluated for an increasing $N$ following the scan order.

Figure 5.35 shows three curves of $v$ related to different subband structures where the peak of the curves just before the steady descent gives the size of the approximation subband. In the current scenario the attacker can also assume that the size of the approximation subband is a power of 2, if the maximum value of the modified variance is not exactly a power of 2, it has to be close to it at least. The fact that this mod-

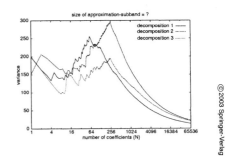

*Figure 5.35.*    Variance for increasing number of coefficients

ified variance is capable of detecting the approximation size has been verified in experiments and so a better (i.e. faster) attacking method can be constructed to detect at first the descending slope by taking a few sample values going "left" until a power of 2 is reached which gives the maximum value.

Once the size of the approximation subband is known, an attacker can get a rough impression of the image but lacks details (compare figure 5.36).

The next step is to reconstruct the remaining decomposition tree which contains the detail subbands. This can be done by exploiting the fact that adjacent lines of coefficients within a subband are correlated since they represent pixels which are situated close to each other. For the subbands in the neighbourhood of the approximation subband there is an upper bound of the size of the subband: the size of the approximation subband. A lower bound exists as well: a subband of size $1 \times 1$ coefficients (in theory), but in practice we may assume the minimum side length to be 2, 4 or even 8 coefficients. Lengths less than 8 are more difficult to cover since in general the amount of data for computing correlations is not big enough. So automatic guesses are not very reliable for small subband sizes, very small subbands usually decrease rate-distortion performance and should be avoided anyway.

In order to determine the size of a subband, we perform a loop ranging from the minimum side length to the maximum side length for the subband in question using subsequent powers of 2. At each step a correlation factor (i.e.

a distance) between adjacent lines of coefficients is computed. Each line is assumed to be a vector of pixels and then the distance between these vectors is calculated. Within this process, we face three situations: We assume a subband size which is smaller than the correct size, we guess the correct size or we assume a size which is larger than the actual size.

In the case we assumed a size which is smaller than the correct size the actual line of coefficients is split into two lines in our subband in testing. When we test the distance a large value is detected. If we assumed the correct size the difference between the lines is smallest.

In the case we assumed a size which is too large we put two lines of the correct subband into one line of our subband. Here we have a correlation as well since consecutive lines in our subband denote alternating lines in the original subband. Therefore, a correlation exists but the

*Figure 5.36.* Reconstruction using a wrong decomposition tree but the correct approximation subband size

distance is higher than in the exact match.

By comparing the distances from several assumed side lengths we can determine the actual size. The iteration step which gives the smallest distance is assumed that it corresponds to the correct match. This iteration is applied recursively to all subbands, the maximum side length is calculated according to the subbands in the neighbourhood. The same process is applied to columns of coefficients as well in order to achieve a higher stability and reliability of the results. Concerning the type of distance measure used, the most promising results were obtained when two $L^i$-norms were used and one of them was the Euclidean norm.

As a consequence, it turns out that our approach is not secure enough when a uniform quantiser is used to encode the coefficients. In most modern wavelet compression methods however more sophisticated coders (as the zerotree coder) are used. These coders require that the encoder and decoder have to be exactly in sync because of the high level of context. In this case the difficulty for attacks is much higher. First investigations show that the complexity is moved near a brute force search for the key used for symmetric encryption. Using a zerotree coder instead of a uniform quantiser has another advantage in general:

the compression rates for a given image quality are better. What can be done in this case to reconstruct the image follows next.

As we have seen, the second option can not be successful in the case of zerotree-based encoding. The stored bits contain more information than actual values, information about significance is stored as well. Additionally, coefficient data is not stored subband oriented but significance oriented. To reconstruct a wavelet packet transformed image using zerotrees the encoder and decoder have to be in perfect synchronisation. This synchronisation is possible just in the case when both parts have the same knowledge about the tree structure. Otherwise the encoder and decoder are out of sync and the bits are interpreted in the wrong way on the decoding end, e.g. bits denoting the significance can be interpreted as sign bits. For an analysis of partial encryption of zerotree encoded imagery see [22].

In the following we investigate option three (exhaustive search for the correct subband structure) in some detail. Equation 5.8 gives the number of possible decomposition trees $f(n)$ reaching up to level $n + 1$.

$$f(n) = \sum_{i=0}^{4} \binom{4}{i} \cdot (f(n-1))^i \qquad (5.8)$$

with $f(0) = 1$ and $a(0) = 1$

For $n = 4$ (5 decomposition levels) this number is in the order of $10^{78}$ or $2^{261}$ which is higher than the complexity of a brute-force attack against encryption using a 256-bit-key AES cipher. But not all subband trees are admissible if a certain compression quality must be guaranteed. Equation 5.9 shows the number of possible decomposition trees $a(n)$ if a minimum and maximum decomposition depth of the approximation subband has been specified. Case (a) has to be applied if the number of decompositions for the approximation subband is below the minimum, (b) is the standard case, and (c) applies when the number of decomposition for the approximation subband reached the maximum.

$$a(n) = \begin{cases} a(n-1) \sum_{i=0}^{3} \binom{3}{i} \cdot (f(n-1))^i & \text{(a)} \\ \sum_{i=0}^{3} \binom{3}{i} \cdot (1 + a(n-1))(f(n-1))^i & \text{(b)} \\ \sum_{i=0}^{3} \binom{3}{i} \cdot (f(n-1))^i & \text{(c)} \end{cases} \qquad (5.9)$$

When restricting the parameters as suggested previously in section we still result in approximately $2^{4185}$ decomposition trees (since the difference to the non-restricted setting is $2^{4120}$ "only"). If the information about restricted parameter ranges is published and further parameters are known to the attacker (like the parameters determining the weight - which should be encrypted anyway), the more probable trees could be tested first. Regarding the vast number of different decomposition trees, attack complexity can not become lower as an attack against 256-bit AES as long as the maximum allowed number of decompositions for all subband is set high enough.

| time(E) | time(P) | Security | BS compl. | BS proc. | affects R/D |
|---------|---------|----------|-----------|----------|-------------|
| low | 0 | high | yes | no | moderately |

*Table 5.21.* Overall assessment of Secret Subband Structures (zerotree variant)

## 2.2 Bitstream Oriented Schemes

### 2.2.1 SPIHT Encryption

Cheng and Li [22] discuss a partial encryption scheme for SPIHT which can be applied to any zerotree-based wavelet coding scheme. The basic observation is as follows: the compression algorithm produces many different types of bits – sign bits, refinement bits, and significance bits of pixels and sets. The decompression algorithm has to interpret each bit under the correct context. Incorrect significance bits may lead to an incorrect interpretation of subsequent bits, this is not the case when sign bits or refinement bits are decoded incorrectly. As a consequence it is suggested to encrypt the significance information of sets and pixels of the two lowest resolution pyramid levels. The reason for not encrypting all significance information is as follows: the significance information of the low resolution levels is used to initialise the different lists used by the algorithm. If the states of these lists are incorrect right from the start of the decoding, it is hardly possible for the algorithm to recover from the error. The information left unencrypted is of low value for an attacker since without the significance information the type of bits can not be distinguished from another. Basically the argumentation is quite similar to the case of encrypting the wavelet packet subband structure only (see last section).

The amount of data encrypted is very small in this proposal – less that 7% in case of $256 \times 256$ pixels images and less than 2% in case of $512 \times 512$ pixels images. The question of bitstream compliance is not discussed, but this property can be easily obtained. Although the methods seems to be very secure, no experimental attacks have been mounted against the scheme proving its robustness.

### 2.2.2 JPEG 2000 Encryption

For selectively encrypting the JPEG 2000 bitstream we have two general options. First, we do not care about the structure of the bitstream and sim-

| time(E) | time(P) | Security | BS compl. | BS proc. | affects R/D |
|---------|---------|----------|-----------|----------|-------------|
| low     | low     | high     | yes       | yes      | no          |

*Table 5.22.*   Overall assessment of SPIHT Encryption

ply encrypt a part, e.g. the first 10% of the bitstream. In this case, the main header and a couple of packets including packet header and packet data are encrypted. Since basic information necessary for reconstruction usually located in the main header is not available at the decoder, encrypted data of this type can not be reconstructed using a JPEG 2000 decoder. Although this seems to be desirable at first sight, an attacker could reconstruct the missing header data using the unencrypted parts, and, additionally, no control over the quality of the remaining unencrypted data is possible. Therefore, the second option is to design a JPEG 2000 bitstream format compliant encryption scheme which does not encrypt main and packet header but only packet data. This option is investigated further.

Grosbois et al. [57] propose the first partial encryption scheme for JPEG 2000 bitstreams. A pseudo random inversion of the bits in certain layers is suggested, but no further details with respect to amount and position of the encrypted data are given. Also, no attacks are demonstrated. Wee and Apostopoulos [172] integrate Motion JPEG 2000 into their secure scalable streaming concept (SSS, compare also section 1.4 (chapter 5)) by exploiting the different ways of achieving scalability in JPEG 2000. Of course, JPEG 2000 suits much better in the SSS context as compared to other codecs since scalability is an inherent property, different mixtures of quality and resolution levels are experimentally evaluated. Triple-DES and AES in CBC mode are used for encryption which means that data has to be padded to suit the block-size specification of these algorithms. A very interesting issue is discussed by Kiya et al. [72] in the context of encrypting packet data of JPEG 2000 streams. Straightforward encryption of this data may lead to the emulation of marker codes which cause the resulting bitstream to be non-compliant and would cause a decoder to crash. They suggest to perform the encryption process based on half bytes in a specific marker aware mode which uses the hexadecimal notation of the markers. Wu and Deng [180] also address the problem of compliant encryption and suggest to check the compliance during the encryption process and to change the process accordingly in case of marker generation. The same authors also discuss an access control scheme using a key generation scheme for parts of the codescheme [181] relying on their former work on hash trees for authenticating JPEG 2000 streams [109].

In the following, we will investigate how much packet data needs to be protected to provide reasonable confidentiality and we will attack a corresponding encryption scheme (compare also [106]). These experiments may be performed online at `http://www.ganesh.org/book/`. We have decided to discuss the encryption efficiency of a JPEG 2000 partial encryption scheme with respect to two different classes of visual image data. The first class of visual data discussed is typical still image data and the testimage representing this class is the Lena image at different resolutions including $256 \times 256$ and $512 \times 512$ pixels. Since this special type of visual data is usually encoded in lossy mode, the lena image is lossy coded in our experiments (at a fixed rate of 2 bpp). The second type of digital visual data should represent an application class where lossless coding is important. We have therefore decided to use an angiogram as testimage in this case (see the corresponding appendix), since angiograms represent an important class of medical image data where lossless coding is usually a mandatory requirement.

In order to make the explanations and experiments of the proposed techniques simpler, we assume the testimages to be given in 8bit/pixel (bpp) precision and in a squared format. Extensions to images of different acquisition types, higher bitdepth or non-squared format are straightforward.

In order to achieve format compliance, we need to access and encrypt data of single packets. Since the aim is to operate directly on the bitstream without any decoding we need to discriminate packet data from packet headers in the bitstream. This can be achieved by using two special JPEG 2000 optional markers which were originally defined to achieve transcoding capability, i.e. manipulation of the bitstream to a certain extent without the need to decode data. Additionally, these markers of course increase error resilience of the bitstream. These markers are "start of packet marker" (SOP - 0xFF91) and "end of packet marker" (EPH - 0xFF92). The packet header is located between SOP and EPH, packet data finally may be found between EPH and the subsequent SOP. For example, using the official JAVA JPEG 2000 reference implementation (JJ2000 - available at `http://jj2000.epfl.ch`) the usage of these markers may be easily invoked by the options -Peph on -Psop on.

Having identified the bitstream segments which should be subjected to encryption we note that packet data is of variable size and does not at all adhere to multiples of a block ciphers block-size. We have to employ AES in CFB mode for encryption, since in this mode, an arbitrary number of data bits can be encrypted, which is not offered by the ECB and CBC encryption modes. Information about the exact specification of the cryptographic techniques used (e.g. key exchange) may be inserted into the JPEG 2000 bitstream taking advantage of so-called termination markers. Parts of the bitstream bounded by termination markers are automatically ignored during bitstream processing and do not interfere with the decoding process. Note that a JPEG 2000 bitstream which is selectively encrypted in the described way is fully compliant to the standard and can therefore be decoded by any codec which adheres to the JPEG 2000 specification.

We want to investigate whether resolution progressive order or layer progressive order is more appropriate for selective JPEG 2000 bitstream encryption. We therefore arrange the packet data in either of the two progression orders, encrypt an increasing number of packet data bytes, reconstruct the images and measure the corresponding quality.

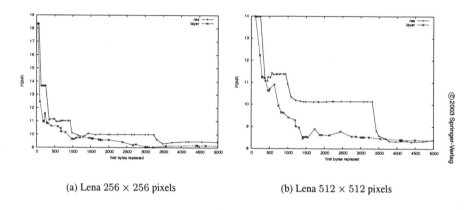

(a) Lena 256 × 256 pixels                    (b) Lena 512 × 512 pixels

*Figure 5.37.*   Comparison of selective encryption (PSNR of reconstructed images) using resolution or layer progressive encoding - part 2.

Resolution progression is more suited for selectively encrypting the angiogram image at higher rates of encrypted data (see Fig. 5.38, where a lower PSNR means that it is more suited for selective encryption). In order to relate the obtained numerical values to visual appearance, two reconstructed versions of the angiogram, corresponding to the two progression orders, are displayed

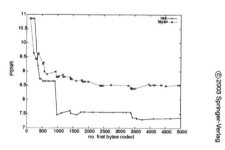

*Figure 5.38.*   Angiogram: Comparison of selective encryption (PSNR of reconstructed images) using resolution or layer progressive encoding - part 1.

in Fig. 5.39. In both cases, 1% of the entire packet data has been encrypted.

Whereas no details are visible using layer progression (Fig. 5.39.a at 8.79 dB), only very high frequency visual information (right lower corner) is visible using resolution progression (Fig. 5.39.b at 7.45 dB).

When considering the Lena image in Fig. 5.37, we observe that resolution progression shows superior PSNR results for both tested image dimensions as compared to layer progression. Two reconstructed versions of the Lena image with $512 \times 512$ pixels, corresponding to the two progression orders, are displayed in Fig. 5.40. In each case, 1% of the entire packet data has been encrypted. Whereas only very high frequency information is visible in the reconstructed image using layer progression (Fig. 5.40.a at 8.51 dB), important visual features are visible using resolution progression (Fig. 5.40.b at 10.11 dB). In this case, the visible high frequency information is enough to reveal sensible data. At 2 % encrypted packet data, this information is destroyed fully in the resolution progressive case.

The Lena image at lower resolution ($256 \times 256$ pixels) performs equally, and the results are therefore only given for the $512^2$ pixels version. Please note also the difference in coarseness of the noise pattern resulting from encryption between resolution and layer progression. Since in resolution progression data corresponding to the higher levels of the wavelet transform is encrypted, the noise introduced by the cipher is propagated by the repeated inverse transform and thereby magnified resulting in a much coarser pattern as compared to layer progression. When summarising the obtained numerical and visual results, it seems that encrypting 1-2% of the packet data in layer progressive mode is sufficient to provide confidentiality for the JPEG 2000 bitstream. This is a very surprising result of course.

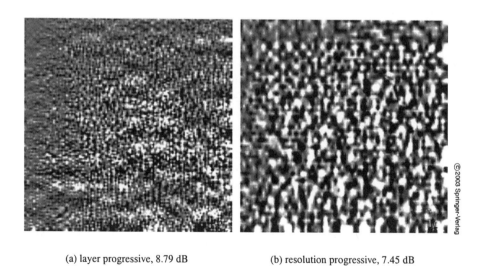

(a) layer progressive, 8.79 dB                    (b) resolution progressive, 7.45 dB

*Figure 5.39.* Comparison of selective encryption (visual quality of reconstructed Angiogram where 1% of the bitstream data have been encrypted) using resolution or layer progressive encoding.

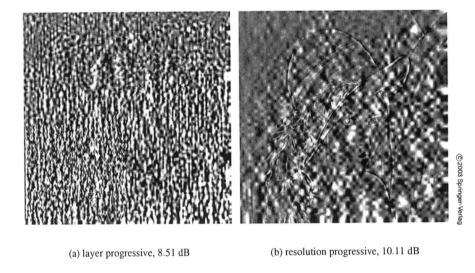

© 2003 Springer-Verlag

(a) layer progressive, 8.51 dB          (b) resolution progressive, 10.11 dB

*Figure 5.40.* Comparison of selective encryption (visual quality of reconstructed Lena (512 pixels) where 1% of the bitstream data have been encrypted) using resolution or layer progressive encoding.

We want to assess the security of the presented selective encryption scheme by conducting a simple ciphertext only attack. Therefore, an attacker would replace the encrypted parts of the bitstream by artificial data mimicking typical images ("replacement attack", see also [112]). This attack is usually performed by replacing encrypted data by some constant bits (i.e. in selective bitplane encryption). In encrypting the JPEG 2000 bitstream, this attack does not have the desired effect, since bitstream values are arithmetically decoded and the corresponding model depends on earlier results and corrupts the subsequently required states. Therefore, the reconstruction result is a noise-like pattern similar as obtained by directly reconstructing the encrypted bitstream. We exploit a built-in error resilience functionality in JJ2000 to simulate a bitstream-based replacement attack. An error resilience segmentation symbol in the codewords at the end of each bit-plane can be inserted. Decoders can use this information to detect and conceal errors. This method is invoked in JJ2000 encoding using the option -Cseg_symbol on.

If an error is detected during decoding (which is of course the case if data is encrypted) it means that the bit stream contains some erroneous bits that have led to the decoding of incorrect data. This data affects the whole last decoded bit-plane. Subsequently, the affected data is concealed and no more passes should be decoded for this code-block's bit stream. The concealment resets the state of the decoded data to what it was before the decoding of the affected bit-plane started. Therefore, the encrypted packets are simply ignored during decoding.

Using this technique, we again compare selective JPEG 2000 encryption using resolution and layer progressive mode layer progressive by reconstructing images with a different amount of encrypted packets. Decoding is done using error concealment. In Fig. 5.41 and 5.42 we immediately recognise that the PSNR values are significantly higher as compared to di-

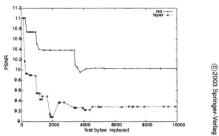

*Figure 5.41.* Angiogram: PSNR of reconstructed images after replacement attack using resolution or layer progressive encoding - part 1.

rectly reconstructed images (see Fig. 5.38 and 5.37). Layer progression is more suited for selectively encrypting the angiogram image. For the lena test images, the situation differs slightly: When encrypting only minor parts of the overall bitstream, layer progression is superior, at higher rates of encryption, the resolution progression scheme shows superior results.

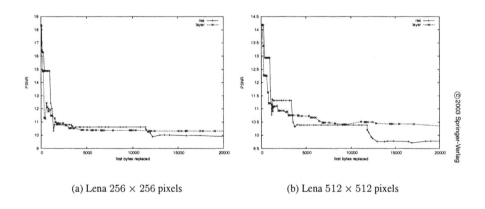

(a) Lena 256 × 256 pixels          (b) Lena 512 × 512 pixels

*Figure 5.42.* PSNR of reconstructed images after replacement attack using resolution or layer progressive encoding - part 2.

Again, the numerical values have to be related to visual inspection. Fig. 5.43.a shows a reconstruction of the selectively compressed angiogram image, where the first 1% of the packets in resolution progressive mode have been encrypted and the reconstruction is done using the error concealment technique. In this case, this leads to a PSNR value of 10.51 dB, whereas the directly reconstructed image has a value of 7.45 dB (see Fig. 5.39.b). The text in the right corner is clearly readable and even the structure of the blood vessels is exhibited. The Lena image performs similarly (see Fig. 5.44.a), all important visual features are reconstructed at 1% encrypted. Here, we have a resulting PSNR of about 11.31 db, whereas the directly reconstructed image has a value of 10.11 dB (see Fig. 5.40.b).

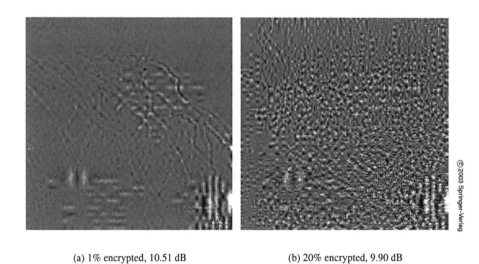

© 2003 Springer-Verlag

(a) 1% encrypted, 10.51 dB                          (b) 20% encrypted, 9.90 dB

*Figure 5.43.* Visual quality of reconstructed Angiogram after replacement attack using resolution encoding.

When increasing the percentage of encrypted packet data steadily, we finally result in 20% percent of the packet data encrypted where neither useful visual nor textual information remains in the image (see Fig. 5.43.b and 5.44.b). This result is confirmed also with other images including other angiograms and other still images and can be used as a rule of thumb for a secure use of selective encryption of the JPEG 2000 bitstream. It has to be noted that the amount of data required to be encrypted is significantly lower in the case of zerotree-based coding schemes. This is due to the higher level (i.e. inter subband) of context information in those coding schemes.

| time(E) | time(P) | Security | BS compl. | BS proc. | affects R/D |
|---|---|---|---|---|---|
| medium+scalable | low | high | yes | no | no |

*Table 5.23.* Overall assessment of JPEG 2000 Encryption

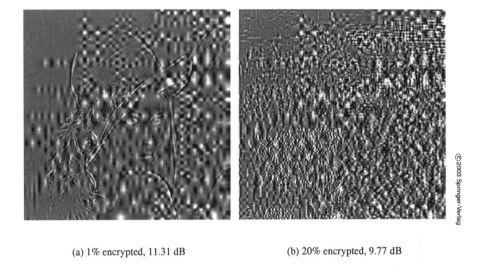

(a) 1% encrypted, 11.31 dB                     (b) 20% encrypted, 9.77 dB

*Figure 5.44.* Visual quality of reconstructed Lena (512 pixels) after replacement attack using resolution encoding.

## 3. Further Techniques

## 3.1 Raw Image Data

### 3.1.1 Permutations

Applying permutations to the raw image data is the simplest and fastest way to apply encryption technology to visual data. Hybrid Pay-TY systems (i.e. analog signal transmission but encryption and decryption is done in the digital domain) have extensively made use of this technology. The Nagravision/Syster system for example applies line permutations within blocks of 32 lines, VideoCrypt (as formerly used by the SKY network) uses specific permutations within each line of the video frame by cutting each line at a secret position and interchanging the two resulting sub-lines. Although the key material is changed frequently, both systems are vulnerable to a ciphertext only attack by using smoothness constraints (guessing a correct permutation results in a smoother image than guessing incorrectly) and known facts about the generation of the permutation keys. Macq and Quisquater [89] propose to use line permutations in the context of a multiresolution image decomposition which facilitates a good control over the amount of degradation. However, this scheme is not more secure than "pure" permutation in the image domain.

| time(E) | time(P) | Security | BS compl. | BS proc. | affects R/D |
|---------|---------|----------|-----------|----------|-------------|
| low     | 0       | low      | yes       | no       | yes         |

*Table 5.24.*   Overall assessment of Permutations applied to raw image data

### 3.1.2    Chaos-based Systems

Chaos-based encryption of visual data uses the principle of applying chaotic maps with strong mixing properties to the raw image data. The basic idea is that (continuous) chaotic maps exhibit similar properties as (discrete) cryptographic systems. Usually, these systems are hybrids between permutation and substitution ciphers with specific properties. Therefore, they are very fast. Scharinger [128] was the first to apply a class of such maps called Kolmogorov flows for this purpose, Fridrich refined and systematised this approach [50, 51]. These algorithms have also been used to conceal logo-type images for watermarking generation [129, 167].

The most famous example of a chaotic map is the "Baker Map" B (defined on $[0,1]^2$) as follows:

$B(x,y) = (2x, y/2)$ for $0 \leq x < 1/2$ and $B(x,y) = (2x - 1, y/2 + 1/2)$ for $1/2 \leq x \leq 1$.

The left vertical half of the domain $[0, 1/2) \times [0, 1)$ is stretched horizontally and contracted vertically to be mapped to the domain $[0, 1) \times [0, 1/2)$. In the same way the right half $[1/2, 1) \times [0, 1)$ is mapped to $[0, 1) \times [1/2, 1)$. Fig. 5.45 illustrates this principle.

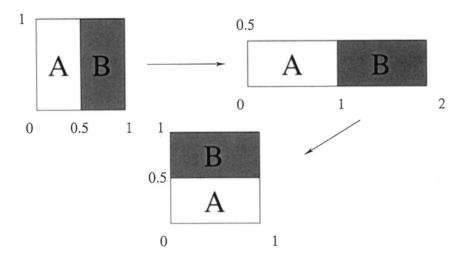

*Figure 5.45.*    Baker Map (1/2,1/2).

The Baker map may be generalised as follows. Instead of processing two halves of the unit interval one considers $k$ vertical rectangles $[F_{i-1}, F_i) \times [0, 1)$ for $i = 1, \ldots, k$ and $F_i = p_1 + p_2 + \cdots + p_i$, $F_0 = 0$, such that $p_1 + \cdots + p_k = 1$. $F_i$ is the left lower corner of rectangle $i$. This generalisation stretches each rectangle horizontally by a factor $1/p_i$ and contracts it vertically by the factor $p_i$. Subsequently, the resulting rectangles are stapled above each other.

In order to be able to apply this map to pixel values, it need to be discretised to a bijection between pixel values. We define a sequence of $k$ positive integers $n_1, \ldots, n_k$ where each $n_i$ divides the width $N$ of a squared image without remainder and $n_1 + \cdots + n_k = N$, $N_i = n_1 + \cdots + n_i$, and $N_0 = 0$. The pixel $(r, s)$ with $N_{i-1} \le r < N_i$ and $0 \le s < N$ is mapped to the following pixel ($q_i = N/n_i$):

$$(q_i(r - N_i) + s \pmod{q)_i}, (s - s \pmod{q)_i}/q_i + N_i).$$

So far, the technique is a pure pixel permutation, defined by the discretised Baker map. The permutation key is the choice of the values for the $n_i$. In order to obtain stronger mixing properties, the map is further generalised to a three dimensional map. A pixel $(r, s)$ with gray value $g_{rs}$ is mapped to $B(r, s)$ with gray value $h(r, s, g_{rs})$ which means that the new gray value depends on pixel position and former gray value. In order to guarantee reversibility, the function $h$ has to be a bijection in the third variable, e.g. $h(r, s, g_{rs}) = g_{rs} + r * s \pmod{L}$ where $L$ is the number of available gray values.

After a low number of iterations (compare Fig. 5.46 which has been generated using J. Scharingers demo page[1]) this technique results in an image with equalised histogram. In order to add diffusion properties, a non-linear feedback shiftregister generator is applied to each column ($g^*_{rs} = g_{rs} + G(g^*_{rs-1})$ $\pmod{L}$ with arbitrary seed). The key material of the entire system consists of the parameters of the chaotic map, the number of iterations, the parameters of the gray value transform $h$, and the values of the shiftregister generator.

| time(E) | time(P) | Security | BS compl. | BS proc. | affects R/D |
|---------|---------|----------|-----------|----------|-------------|
| low | 0 | medium-high | yes | no | yes |

*Table 5.25.* Overall assessment of Chaotic Encryption

For more information and a detailed description of various flavours of this techniques please refer to Chapter 4 of the Multimedia Security Handbook [54].

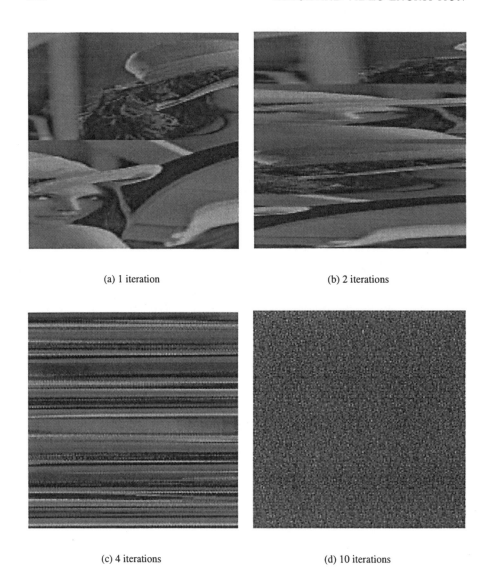

(a) 1 iteration                                (b) 2 iterations

(c) 4 iterations                               (d) 10 iterations

*Figure 5.46.*    Baker Map (1/2,1/2) applied to Lena.

### 3.1.3    Bitplane Encryption

For the results in this section see also [104, 112]. For simplicity, we assume
an $512 \times 512$ pixels image to be given in 8bit/pixel (bpp) precision. We consider the 8bpp data in the form of 8 bitplanes, each bitplane associated with a
position in the binary representation of the pixels. The encryption approach is

to e.g. AES encrypt a subset of the bitplanes only, starting with the bitplane containing the most significant bit (MSB) of the pixels. Each possible subset of bitplanes may be chosen for encryption, however, the minimal percentage of data to be encrypted is 12.5 % (when encrypting the MSB bitplane only), increasing in steps of 12.5 % for each additional bitplane encrypted. We use an AES implementation with blocksize 128 bit and a 128 bit key. The 128 bit block is filled with a quarter of a bitplane line ($512/4 = 128$ bits). The encrypted bitplanes are transmitted together with the remaining bitplanes in plain text.

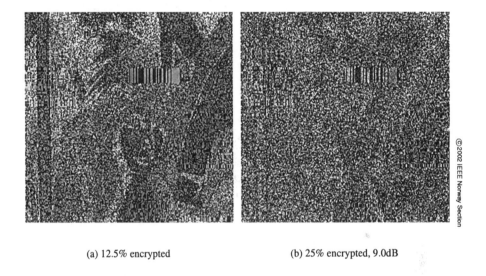

© 2002 IEEE Norway Section

(a) 12.5% encrypted    (b) 25% encrypted, 9.0dB

*Figure 5.47.*    Visual examples for selective bitplane encryption, direct reconstruction.

Fig. 5.47 shows two examples of directly reconstructed images after selectively encrypting 1 and 2 bitplane(s). Whereas in the case of encrypting the MSB only structural information is still visible, encrypting two bitplanes leaves no useful information in the reconstruction, at least when directly reconstructing the image data.

Note the pattern reminiscent of a bar code in the upper right quarter of the image. Fig. 5.48.a shows the encrypted MSB of the Lena image where this pattern is exhibited even clearer. This phenomenon is due to the fact that AES encryption is used with identical key for all blocks in the image. Consequently, if there are identical plain text quarter-lines directly situated above each other which also adhere to the AES block-border (i.e. starting at pixel positions 0, 128, 256, or 384), these data produce identical ciphertext blocks. Identical blocks of ciphertext are again arranged as identical quarter-lines thereby generating the barcode effect. For the corresponding region with identical quarter-lines starting at pixel position 128 in the MSB of the Lena image refer to Fig. 5.51.a.

(a) encrypted MSB                        (b) 50% encrypted, 31.8dB

*Figure 5.48.*    Further visual examples for selective bitplane encryption.

Note that it is of course important to encrypt the MSB first and continue with the bitplanes corresponding to the next bits in the binary representation. Fig. 5.48.b shows the case where the image is directly reconstructed after 4 bitplanes have been encrypted starting from the least significant bit (LSB). Almost no degradation is visible here – consequently it hardly makes any sense at all to encrypt these data. Table 5.26 gives the PSNR values of images subjected to the SE approach. Whereas the PSNR is constant 9 dB when encrypting the MSB first, PSNR decreases steadily from 51 dB to 14 dB for each additional bitplane encrypted and reaches 9 dB when encrypting all bitplanes after all in the case when the LSB bitplane is encrypted first.

| # Bitplanes | 1 | 2 | 3 | 4 | 5 | 6 | 7 | 8 |
|---|---|---|---|---|---|---|---|---|
| First: LSB | 51 | 44 | 38 | 32 | 26 | 20 | 14 | 9 |
| First: MSB | 9 | 9 | 9 | 9 | 9 | 9 | 9 | 9 |

*Table 5.26.*   PSNR of images after direct reconstruction related to the number of encrypted bitplanes and to the ordering of the bitplanes.

A technique to eventually increase the security could be not to disclose which bitplanes have been subjected to encryption besides the MSB. Fig. 5.49

shows directly reconstructed images where the MSB and n-th most significant bitplanes have been encrypted. Clearly, the visual quality is comparable to encrypting the MSB alone (compare Fig. 5.47.a).

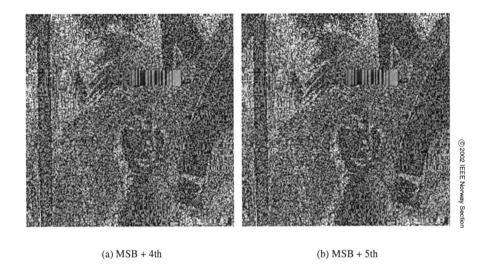

(a) MSB + 4th  (b) MSB + 5th

*Figure 5.49.* Visual examples for encryption of MSB and one additional bitplane.

Additionally, the statistical properties of bitplanes of natural images and encrypted bitplanes are fairly different. Table 5.27 compares the number of runs consisting of 5 identical bits contained in bitplanes (plaintext and ciphertext). All but the three less significant bitplanes show a much higher value of runs in the plaintext version. Therefore, the "secret" which bitplanes have been encrypted can be immediately solved using simple statistics.

| Bitplane | MSB | 2 | 3 | 4 | 5 | 6 | 7 | LSB |
|---|---|---|---|---|---|---|---|---|
| Plain | 45 | 39 | 32 | 20 | 11 | 5 | 4 | 4 |
| Encrypted | 4 | 4 | 4 | 4 | 4 | 4 | 4 | 4 |

*Table 5.27.* Number of runs consisting of 5 identical bits (rounded to thousand, Lena image).

As a consequence, the most secure way to perform selective bitplane encryption is to encrypt the MSB bitplane and subsequently additional bitplanes in the order of decreasing significance with respect to their position in the binary representation.

In the following we assess the security of selective bitplane encryption by conducting two types of simple ciphertext only attacks. A shortcoming of many investigations of visual data encryption is the lack of quantifying the quality of the visual data that can be obtained by attacks against encryption. Mostly visual examples are provided only. The reason is the poor correlation of PSNR and other simple quality measures and perceived quality especially for low-quality images [143]. Note for example that the PSNR computed between the image Lena and its entirely AES encrypted version is 9.2 dB whereas PSNR between Lena and an image with constant grayvalue 128 is 14.5 dB ! Both images do not carry any structural information related to Lena, however, the PSNR values differ more than 5 dB. For the most simple attack we may even relate the visual examples to meaningful numerical values.

Assuming the cipher in use is unbreakable we conduct the first attack by directly reconstructing the selectively encrypted images. The encrypted parts introduce noise-type distortions (see Fig. 5.47). Therefore, we replace the encrypted parts by artificial data mimicking typical images. The encrypted bit-plane is replaced by a constant 0 bitplane and the resulting decrease in average luminance is compensated by adding 64 to each pixel if only the MSB bitplane was encrypted, 96 if the MSB and next bitplane have been encrypted, and so on. Subsequently, reconstruction is performed as usual, treating the encrypted and replaced parts as being non-encrypted.

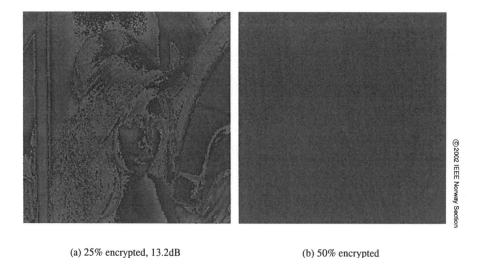

(a) 25% encrypted, 13.2dB                                    (b) 50% encrypted

*Figure 5.50.*    Visual examples for the efficiency of the Replacement Attack.

Fig. 5.50 shows two visual examples of image reconstructions as obtained by the Replacement Attack (2 and 4 bitplanes are encrypted). Whereas a direct reconstruction of an image with 2 bitplanes encrypted suggests this setting to be "safe" (with 9.0dB quality, see Fig. 5.47.b), the Replacement Attack reveals that structural information is still present in the reconstructed image (with 13.2dB quality, see Fig. 5.50.a). However, the visual information is severely alienated. Obviously, not only the visual appearance but also the numerical PSNR values have been significantly improved by the Replacement Attack. In any case, even if a Replacement Attack is mounted, encrypting 4 bitplanes (i.e. 50% of the original data) leads to perfectly satisfying results (Fig. 5.50.b).

For the simplest case of this encryption technique, we assume the MSB bitplane to be encrypted only. The idea of the *Reconstruction Attack* is to reconstruct the MSB data with the aid of the unencrypted remaining data. We exploit the well known property, that most regions of natural images are covered by areas with smoothly changing gray values (except edges, of course). In areas of this type, the MSBs of all pixels tend to be identical (except for the case of medium luminance). In order to automatically detect such areas we define a 2 × 2 pixels search window in which all 16 possible combinations of MSB configurations are tested. In this test, a certain set of differences among the 4 pixel values is computed for each of the 16 MSB configurations. Out of the set of differences, the smallest difference is selected and the corresponding configuration of the MSB bits in the search window is defined to be the reconstruction. Fig. 5.51.a shows the MSB of the Lena image and Fig. 5.51.b a reconstructed bitplane obtained as described above.

(a) original MSB          (b) reconstructed bitplane

*Figure 5.51.* MSB of the Lena image and reconstructed Bitplane.

It is clearly visible that smooth areas are satisfactorily recovered (black=0) whereas edges are represented by white lines. This "edge-detection capability" is due to the fact that when the search window hits an edge, the difference operation leads to an attempt to compensate thereby setting the MSB to different values at both sides of the edge. Fig. 5.52 shows an image (index=1) resulting from the Reconstruction Attack where about 50% of the smooth areas are recovered correctly. A second difference exists with equally low value which is obtained as well by setting all MSB values constant (white=1) in smooth areas. Using this as additional information, a second reconstruction is obtained where the remaining 50% of the smooth areas are recovered correctly (see Fig. 5.52 – index=2).

When combining these two reconstructed "half-images" the original may be obtained easily by choosing the correct areas from the respective half-images (see Fig. 5.52).

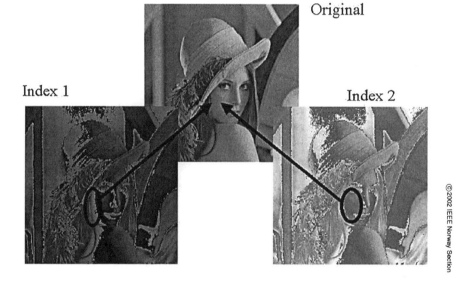

*Figure 5.52.*    Combination of two half-images after Reconstruction Attack.

However, the complexity of this attack increases significantly if more bit-planes are encrypted and also the reliability of the results is drastically reduced. Summarising it seems that a relatively high amount of data needs to be encrypted to achieve reasonable security.

| time(E) | time(P) | Security | BS compl. | BS proc. | affects R/D |
|---------|---------|----------|-----------|----------|-------------|
| high | low | low-medium | yes | no | yes |

*Table 5.28.*    Overall assessment of Bitplane Encryption

## 3.2    Quadtrees

Quadtree compression partitions the visual data into a structural part (the quadtree structure) and colour information (the leave values). Cheng et al. [21, 22, 82] suggest to encrypt the quadtree structure only and to keep the leave values in plaintext. As it is the case with wavelet packets (see section 2.1.4 (chapter 5)) a brute-force attack is not feasible due to the exceedingly high number of possible quadtrees. The only way to attack such a scheme is to try to deduce the quadtree structure from the non-encrypted leave values. In this context, the authors discuss two variants how the leave values may be organised in the compressed file (i.e. scan order, Fig. 5.53 shows an example for each of the orderings):

1  Leaf ordering I: is a depth first scan which starts with the NW quadrant, counterclockwise.

2  Leaf ordering II: is a line oriented scan within each level of the quadtree, starting with the smallest leaves.

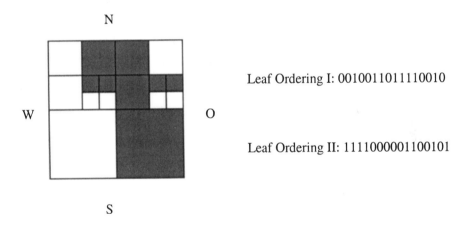

Leaf Ordering I: 0010011011110010

Leaf Ordering II: 1111000001100101

*Figure 5.53.*    Example for leaf ordering I and II.

It turns out there exists an attack against leaf ordering I whereas ordering II seems to be secure. The problem with leaf ordering I is that leaves which are neighbours in the quadtree are also neighbours in the bitstream. Based on this observation one notices that runs (i.e. a sequence of identical leave values) provide information about the local quadtree structure, since four identical adjacent leave values can never be situated at the same quadtree level (in this case no quadtree partitioning would have taken place). These facts may be exploited to significantly reduce the admissible quadtrees during an attack.

In case of lossy quadtree compression, the quadtree structure covers about 15 – 25 % of the entire data. Therefore, a significant amount of data needs

| time(E) | time(P) | Security | BS compl. | BS proc. | affects R/D |
|---------|---------|----------|-----------|----------|-------------|
| high    | high    | high     | -         | yes      | no          |

*Table 5.29.*   Overall assessment of Quadtree Encryption

to be encrypted. If the data is not given in quadtree compressed form (which is highly probable), the complexity of compression needs to be considered as well.

The authors also suggest to encode and subsequently encrypt motion vector fields using quadtrees. This can be done in identical manner, however, it has to be taken into account that size of the corresponding motion vector frames is rather small and the size of the keyspace (i.e. number of admissible quadtrees) may be rather small as well.

## 3.3    Fractal-based system

Roche et al. [125] propose an access control system for fractal encoded visual data which may be operated ranging from a full encryption mode to a variant where the images are only slightly distorted ("transparent encryption", see section 4 (chapter 5)). The main idea is to partially encrypt the binary representation of the luminance scale parameter. Whereas reconstruction or filtering of the corrupted image data is extremely difficult due to the highly non-linear distortions induced by fractal interpolation, the amount of parsing to extract the data subjected to encryption is significant. Further, due to the robustness of the decoding process, this technique is hardly useful to provide real confidentiality. Transparent encryption may be a better application field.

| time(E) | time(P) | Security | BS compl. | BS proc. | affects R/D |
|---------|---------|----------|-----------|----------|-------------|
| low     | high    | low      | yes       | yes      | no          |

*Table 5.30.*   Overall assessment of Encrypting Fractal Encoded Data

## 3.4    Vector quantisation based system

Chen et al. [20] propose a very interesting image encryption system which is actually a hybrid between image encryption and image steganography. It is called a "virtual image cryptosystem". Using terminology from information hiding [68] a cover image is used to embed the image to be encrypted. The embedding stage is performed using a vector quantisation codebook which is derived from both the cover image and the image to be protected. The security relies on the fact that two random vectors are encrypted in secure manner, concatenated repeatedly to generate a keystream which is then XORed with the list of indices from vector quantisation. This simple scheme is of course a threat for the security of the system. Secure encryption of the entire list of indices would be the other choice, however, computational amount for this operation is significant. We rate the second approach only.

| time(E) | time(P) | Security | BS compl. | BS proc. | affects R/D |
|---------|---------|----------|-----------|----------|-------------|
| medium | high | high | yes | no | no |

*Table 5.31.* Overall assessment of the Virtual Image Cryptosystem

## 3.5 Base-switching based system

Chang and Lin [24] use a recent lossless image codec for their encryption scheme. After partitioning the image into $3 \times 3$ pixels blocks these blocks are transformed involving the "base value" which is the difference between maximum and minimum of the pixel values in the blocks. The authors assume that this value stays in the range $[1, 128]$ and the security of the entire system resides in encrypting this base value. Without having access to the base value the remaining data for each block cannot be decoded and the field containing the base value for the next block cannot be identified. Although it is claimed that there would be 128! mappings from the plain base value to the encrypted one, a brute-force attack only requires 128 guesses per block to test all possible base values. Taking into account several plausibility criteria, an attack could probably be mounted with much less effort. Regarding this observation, taken together with the fact that the compression scheme is not very effective and hardly ever used, the system does not seem to be very practical. Additionally this method is susceptible to known plaintext attacks because then the attacker knows the encrypted und the unencrypted version of the base value, so that the following bits can be interpreted without a chance of error.

## 4. Transparent Encryption

Macq and Quisquater [89, 90] introduce the term transparent encryption mainly in the context of digital TV broadcasting: a broadcaster of pay TV does not always intend to prevent unauthorised viewers from receiving and watching his program, but rather intends to promote a contract with nonpaying watchers. This can be facilitated by providing a low quality version of the broadcasted program for everyone, only legitimate (paying) users get access to the full quality visual data. This is meant also by the term "try and buy" scenario. Therefore, privacy is not the primary concern in such an environment.

Transparent encryption aims at protecting the details of the data which enable a pleasant viewing experience in an efficient manner. If this data are missing, the user is (hopefully) motivated to pay for the rest of the data. Another application area are preview images in image and video databases.

Transparent encryption can be implemented in various ways. The simplest approach is to use any arbitrary selective encryption scheme and to restrict the amount of data encrypted in a way that the visual information content is still perceivable. However, in many cases the quality of the data will be too bad to be useful in the context of transparent encryption. Consequently, techniques specifically tailored to the transparent encryption scenario have been developed.

As already briefly mentioned in section 3.1.1 (chapter 5), Macq and Quisquater [89] propose to use line permutations in the transform domain of a lossless multiresolution transform. The permutations are only applied in the region of the transform domain corresponding to fine grained details of the data. Droogenbroeck and Benedett [39] propose to encrypt bitplanes of the binary representation of raw image data, contrasting to the privacy focused approach discussed in section 3.1.3 they suggest to start with the LSB bitplane. With respect to JPEG encoded images, the authors suggest to encrypt sign and magnitude bits of medium and high frequency DCT coefficients (note that this is exactly just the other way round as compared to the Scalable Coefficient Encryption algorithm in section 1.1.1 where low frequency coefficients are encrypted only). Droogenbroeck [38] extends this latter idea to "multiple encryption" where different sets of DCT coefficients are encrypted by different content owners, and "over encryption" where these sets do not have an empty intersection (i.e. coefficients are encrypted twice or even more often). Also spatial selective encryption is discussed. The standalone encryption of motion vectors has found to be too weak for privacy focused encryption (see section 1.2.1). Bodo et al. [17] propose a technique called "waterscrambling" where they embed a watermark into the motion vectors of an MPEG stream. In particular, the suggest to DCT transform the motion vector field and to add a watermark using a robust (secret) spread spectrum technique. The high robustness of the scheme leads to the desired side effect that the video is distorted, only a legitimate user has access to the key and may descramble the motion vectors.

Transparent encryption may be implemented in the most efficient way in the context of scalable or embedded bitstreams. As already mentioned in section 1.4, transparent encryption is achieved in this environment by simply encrypting the enhancement layer(s). This has been proposed by Kunkelmann and Horn using a scalable video codec based on a spatial resolution pyramid [76, 75] and by Dittmann and Steinmetz [35, 36] using a SNR scalable MPEG-2 encoder/decoder (compare section 1.4). Yuan et al. [182] finally propose to use MPEG-4 FGS for transparent encryption, where contrasting to the previous approaches several enhancement layers are suggested to be used.

## 5.     Commercial Applications and Standards

### 5.1     JPSEC — secure JPEG 2000

JPSEC will be a standard also known as ISO/IEC 15444-8, it is an extension to the JPEG-2000 standard. According to the current timeline [133, resolution 42] we can expect the FDIS (Final Draft International Standard) in December 2004, and the final standard in February 2005. Since JPSEC is not finalised at the time of this writing the following information might change.

JPSEC allows the content creators and providers to protect parts (called "zone of influence" ZOI) of a JPSEC file. It distinguishes between image data and non-image data (e.g. headers), and it allows manifold protection schemes: fragile integrity verification (using cryptographic hashes), semi-fragile verification (usually with the help of watermarks), source authentication, conditional access, secure scalable streaming and transcoding, registered content identification and of course confidentiality (by encryption or selective encryption). JPSEC allows multiple applications of the above protection methods on the same data, for example it will be possible during creation to first authenticate the image, watermark it, and then to encrypt a part of it. On the side of the recipient the process is then reversed. Some protection methods are predefined (such as encryption using AES), but others can be attached. The standardisation committee decided to set up a registry for such additional protection methods, such a registry allows the unique identification of the protection methods in any JPSEC bitstream.

### 5.2     IPMP — Intellectual Property Management and Protection

IPMP is a standard within the MPEG family which has been developed at first for MPEG-2 and MPEG-4. During the time some problems with this version of the standard have been found (there were interoperability conflicts with security and with flexibility). A second attempt, now part of MPEG-21 ("Multimedia Framework") tries to address the wishes of consumers and manufacturers, this new version was "back-ported" to MPEG-2 and -4, and can be found there as IPMP-X.

IPMP tries to create a way of interoperability for the deployment of content and applications, it distinguishes between 5 different communities: end-users or consumers, content providers, device manufacturers, service providers, and content authors. IPMP tries to meet the goals of all these groups by the creation of an extensive framework. One important part of this framework is the concept of the "IPMP tools": they are modules that perform one or more functions like authentication, decryption or watermarking on an IPMP terminal, such modules are identified by an ID, they can be embedded in a bitstream, downloaded or acquired by other means. When a user requests a specific content, then the following steps are executed: the IPMP tools description is accessed, the relevant IPMP tools are retrieved, instantiated, initialised and updated during the content consumption [71, 98].

For working documents and information about the availability of finished standards please go to the official MPEG home page[2], for some open-source code which implements IPMP you might want to visit sourceforge[3] or use your favourite search engine.

## 5.3    MPEG, DVB & CSA

ETSI (European Telecommunications Standards Institute) says in their DVB cookbook [45, section 4]:

> In many cases DVB-based services will either be of the pay type or will at least include some elements which are not supposed to be freely available to the public at large. The term Conditional Access is frequently used to describe systems that enable the control over the access to programmes, services etc.
>
> Conditional Access (CA) systems consist of several blocks; among others, the mechanism to scramble the programme or service, the Subscriber Management System (SMS), in which all customer data are stored and the Subscriber Authorisation System (SAS), that encrypts and delivers those code words which enable the descrambler to make the programme legible.

In this book we focus on the actual image or video compression and encryption methods, so we leave out most of the surrounding framework and infrastructure. Several approaches exist to encrypt MPEG data, some comply to existing standards, others do not. Betacrypt is an example for the latter, it was based on a first version of Irdeto, but Betacrypt seems to be gone (due to various reasons, e.g. provider bankruptcy, or successful piracy). Other encryption schemes are Simulcrypt and Multicrypt:

Simulcrypt allows the use of multiple set-top boxes, each with its own CA system. The CA system (sometimes also called CAM = conditional access module) that received codes that this module recognises then performs the decryption. Multicrypt allows several CA systems to coexist in the same set-top box, usually using PCMCIA slots (CI = common interface) to plug them into the box, the MPEG data is sent to all (that is usually: both) modules in sequence. Some literature sometimes also mentions Equicrypt with references to [58] or [80], but it seems that this method did not evolve beyond project status[4].

The MPEG standards include an encryption mechanism which allows vendor-specific plugins, it is called "Common Scrambling Algorithm" CSA. CSA is built as a combination of a block cipher and a stream cipher. The block cipher uses a 64-bit key to generate 56 different 64-bit keys for the individual rounds to encrypt a 64-bit block. The stream cipher uses several LFSRs in parallel, each 10 bits long, the output is fed back via an S-box permutation. During decryption the data is first decrypted using the stream cipher and then by the block cipher.

The algorithm was secret for several years, it was build just in hardware. Some information about it can be obtained from two patents [13, 12]. Eventually some software leaked into the internet, the binary (FreeDec) has been reverse-engineered and so the code became public. Some sites on the internet contain information about it, an example is http://csa.irde.to/ .

The idea is that every provider uses the same algorithm to encrypt the transmitted MPEG stream. Each provider can use its own algorithm to calculate the seed value for CSA. On the customer side the MPEG-receiver needs a "Conditional Access Module" from the respective provider which enables the decryption. Modern receivers contain an interface following the "Common Interface Standard", such an interface is basically a PCMCIA slot, and the access module (also called "CI module") is a smartcard within a PCMCIA adapter. The chip on the smartcard is responsible for the correct generation of the CSA seed values. This seed is also called "Control Word" or "Common Key".

In the following we list some commercial systems, some of them provide conditional access to video within the framework specified above, others do not, but they rarely publish detailed information about the inner workings of their products. However, most claim that their systems comply to the DVB standard.

**Conax:** a Telenor-offspring, see http://www.conax.com/

**Cryptoworks:** provided by Philips, see http://www.software.philips.com/↩
InformationCenter/Global/FHomepage-NoXCache.asp?lNodeId=866 .

**Irdeto:** Irdeto Access, originally based in the Netherlands, is a subsidiary of the international subscriber platform group MIH Limited, which is a subsidiary of Naspers. See http://www.irdetoaccess.com/

**Mediaguard:** sometimes also referred to as "SECA" (Societe Europeene de Controle d'Acces), developed by Nagra France, a part of the Kudelski Group. see http://www.nagra.fr/

**Nagravision:** another descendant of the Kudelski Group, see http://www.nagravision.com/

**Viaccess:** a     member     of     the     France     Telecom     group,
`http://www.viaccess.fr/index_solutions.html`

**Videoguard:** provided by NDS, see `http://www.nds.com/`

Using this two-stage encryption schemes gives two points of possible attacks: CSA, and the individual CI modules. Currently there exists no attacks on CSA, at least no attacks that are known in the public. Such an attack would be fatal: due to its nature it would allow to circumvent all the individual encryption schemes. This lack of an attack can be explained by two different reasons: first, the cipher is good enough to withstand all the attacks from cryptographers around the world. And second, nobody cares to attack the cipher. Since the cipher is used to protect multimedia content and since it is the commercial basis of some content providers one can assume that there are other forces which might have opposite interests. Therefore option two is unlikely.

The second class of attacks is directed against individual providers and their CI modules. The smartcards are handed out to the customers and therefore they must be considered to be in enemy territory. The providers take precautions against dissection of such smartcards, but in some cases pirates were successful.

## 5.4   DVD

DVDs can be protected using an encryption method called CSS, which was developed in 1996 by Matsushita. The sectors of such a DVD are encrypted using a chain of keys:

**Title keys:** these keys are used to protect the actual contents on the DVD.

**Disc keys:** these keys are used to encrypt/decrypt the title keys on the DVD.

**Player keys:** these keys are used to protect the access to the disc keys. The disc key is stored 400-fold in encrypted form on the DVD, each time encrypted with a different player key. Each DVD player manufacturer gets its own player key, the manufacturer must take care because it must not be compromised.

To access a title on a DVD the player has to use its own key to decrypt the disc key. This disc key is used to obtain the title key for a specific title on the DVD. Prior to this encryption sequence the DVD drive and the unit performing the CSS decryption have to authenticate to each other, to verify that the partner module complies with the DVD standards. DVD copy protection mechanisms are described in more detail in [16].

Suddenly in 1999 a software tool called "DeCSS" appeared on the net and spread like a virus. It was a tool which enabled to view, read and copy encrypted DVDs on computers. This feature was desperately needed because the

DVD player manufactures focused on mainstream operating systems but neglected others, like the emerging masses of Linux systems. Without official support the users had to build their own DVD players.

Soon a person was identified who should be responsible for this tool: Jon Johansen. In 2002 Johansen was accused of distributing a copyright circumvention technique, but the appellate court in Oslo, Norway, confirmed the ruling of the first instance court that he is not guilty. Some, for instance the US film industry, claim that Johansen is the author of DeCSS, others say that he was just a front man. Details can be found in a document floating around in the internet titled "The Truth about DVD CSS cracking by MoRE and [dEZZY/DoD]" [5].

After the spreading of DeCSS the DVD CCA (Copy Control Association) was founded, this group is now responsible for the licensing of CSS, details can be obtained from their web-pages, e.g. `http://www.dvdcca.org/css/`.

Besides the use of DeCSS to crack CSS, CSS also contains some weaknesses which allow a brute-force attack to get access within a reasonable time. The first weakness is its short key, 40 bits, this is way too short for current cryptosystems. See as an example the web site `http://www.distributed.net/`: The RC5 56-bit challenge was completed within 250 days, 40 bits are a $\frac{1}{65536}$ of work. Also take into account that the computing hardware advanced tremendously: in one formulation Moores law predicts that the processing power doubles every 18 months, this also means that the expected time to crack a cipher by brute-force is reduced by a factor of 2. RC5-56 was completed in 1997, this means that the processing power is 16-fold in 2003 and the expectations are that in 2006 the number will be 64.

Another weakness is the use of LFSRs, depending on the actual attack the knowledge of 5 or 6 bytes of output of the LFSRs is sufficient to obtain the key. Stevenson shows another attack, this time the target is the hash of the disk key, with an attack complexity of $2^{25}$ [147], recall from above that a stupid brute-force attack has complexity $2^{40}$. An overview and a collection of these weaknesses was written by Greg Kesden[6].

## 5.5 Other commercial products

This section includes companies and products which do not suit into the categories above, e.g. because such a product scrambles *analog* video data, most products are for CCTV purposes. The information provided here cannot be complete since companies and products come and go. The information is provided as-is and should not be considered a recommendation.

- Mel Secure Systems Ltd provides a product "Imagelock" for video encryption/scrambling.
  See `http://www.melsecuresystems.co.uk/imagelock.html`

- SLD Security & Communications sells TeleGuard for video transmission via radio.
  See `http://teleguard.biz/products/videotx/digitalradio.htm`

- Verint seems to sell video systems from different producers, including CCTV systems with encrypted wireless transmission.
  See `http://www.verint.com/video_solutions/`

- Ovation Systems produce various video encryption or scrambling systems, online at `http://www.ovation.co.uk/Products/products.html`

- Tango Systems, Inc. produces systems for video transmission.
  See `http://www.trangosys.com/products/Overview.cfm`

- and many more ...

## Notes

1 `http://www.cast.uni-linz.ac.at/Research/DIP/ImageEncryption/bernoulli.html`

2 currently at `http://www.chiariglione.org/mpeg/`

3 `http://sourceforge.net/projects/openipmp/`

4 `http://www.cordis.lu/infowin/acts/rus/projects/ac051.htm`

5 from e.g. `http://www-2.cs.cmu.edu/%7Edst/DeCSS/MoRE+DoD.txt`

6 available at `http://www-2.cs.cmu.edu/%7Edst/DeCSS/Kesden/`

# Chapter 6

# CONCLUSIONS

Image and video encryption is neither in its infancy nor it may be considered a mature technique. On the one hand, many proposals exist with respect to possible technologies and we have learned a lot since the first suggestions have been published in the mid-nineties:

- There are better ways to achieve confidentiality for visual data than to AES encrypt the corresponding bitstream in case security is not the only criterion for successful deployment.

- The "There is nor free lunch" theorem also applies to encryption of visual data. Whereas encryption effort may be significantly reduced by employing selective techniques, bitstream compliance may not be achieved in a simple and time-efficient manner easily.

- Visual data in scalable formats may be encrypted much more efficiently and with much better functionalities. In particular, selective encryption can be performed efficiently only when applied to scalable or embedded bitstreams.

- Highly context-based wavelet compression schemes seem to be better suited for selective encryption as compared to classical DCT based compression schemes like MPEG or JPEG.

On the other hand, international standards representing state of the art like MPEG IPMP or JPSEC are quite recent or not even finalized. Commercial products like DVD or many Pay-TV systems mostly base their security policies on the "security by obscurity" principle and have consequently been successfully attacked.

Consequently, we will see interesting developments in this area in the near future. In particular, with respect to real-world usage it will be interesting to see if the entertainment and telecommunication industries will make extensive use of the new standards MPEG IPMP and JPSEC. From the more research oriented perspective, the integration and interoperability of different multimedia security techniques (e.g. encryption and robust watermarking or encryption and fragile watermarking) poses a huge amount of open questions. Therefore, this field is expected to remain exciting for some time.

# Appendix A
# Copyrighted sections

The following listing gives information about sections of this monograph which have been previously published and are therefore partially copyrighted by other publishers.

| Chapter | Section no. | Copyright | Reference |
|:---:|:---:|:---:|:---:|
| 4 | 1 | EURASIP | [123] |
| 4 | 2 | ACM | [114] |
| 4 | 3 | EURASIP | [123] |
| 5 | 1.4.1 | EURASIP | [46] |
| 5 | 2.1.2 | IEEE Sig.Proc.Soc. | [105] |
| 5 | 2.1.4 | IEEE Sig.Proc.Soc. | [113] |
|  |  | IEEE | [73] |
|  |  | ACM | [118] |
|  |  | Springer-Verlag | [117] |
| 5 | 2.2.2 | Springer-Verlag | [106] |
| 5 | 3.1.3 | IEEE Norway Section | [112] |

# Appendix B
# Test Images and Videos

## 1. Cover Page

## 2. Test Images

These eight test images have been used in some experiments throughout this book: Lena, Baboon (sometimes also denoted Mandrill), Angiogram, Claire (which is actually frame 0 of the corresponding test video), Lung (a lung CT), Plane, Graves, and Barbara.

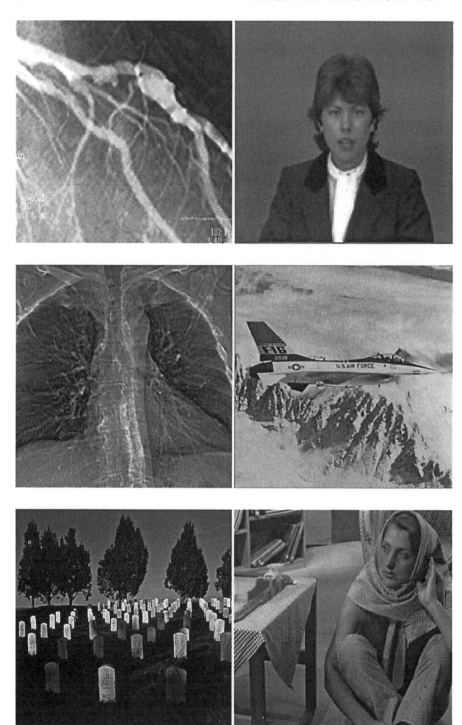

## 3.　Sequence 1 — Bowing

This sequence consists of 300 frames, each with 352*288 colour pixels.

## 4.　Sequence 2 — Surf Side

This sequence consists of 17 frames, each with 720*576 grayscale pixels.

## 5.　Sequence 3 — Coast Guard

This sequence consists of 300 frames, each with 176*144 colour pixels.

# 6.    Sequence 4 — Akiyo

This sequence consists of 300 frames, each with 176*144 colour pixels.

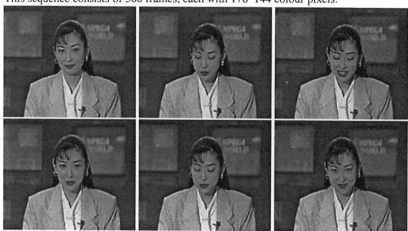

# 7.    Sequence 5 — Calendar

This sequence consists of 300 frames, each with 352*288 colour pixels.

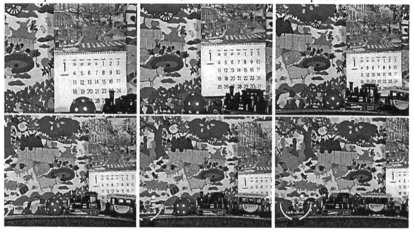

# Appendix C
# Authors' Biographies

## Andreas Uhl

*Andreas Uhl* received the B.S. and M.S. degrees (both in Mathematics) from Salzburg University and he completed his PhD on Applied Mathematics at the same University. He is currently associate professor with tenure in computer science affiliated with the Department of Scientific Computing. He is also part-time lecturer at the Carinthia Tech Institute and has been a guest professor at Linz and Klagenfurt universities recently. His research interests include multimedia signal processing (with emphasis on compression and security issues), parallel and distributed processing, and numbertheoretical methods in numerics.

## Andreas Pommer

*Andreas Pommer* received his degrees in computer science also from the University of Salzburg. He works as an assistant professor at the department of Scientific Computing at the University of Salzburg. Research interests include but are not limited to security of computer systems and networks, high performance computing and various aspects of multimedia.

# References

[1] 3GPP Organizational Partners. Specification of the 3GPP confidentiality and integrity algorithms — document 2: KASUMI specification, December 1999. available online from http://portal.etsi.org/dvbandca/3GPP/3gppspecs.asp.

[2] 3GPP Organizational Partners. Specification of the 3GPP confidentiality and integrity algorithms — document 1: f8 and f9 specification, version 1.2, September 2000. available online from http://portal.etsi.org/dvbandca/3GPP/3gppspecs.asp.

[3] H. Abut, editor. *Vector Quantization*. New York: IEEE Press, 1990.

[4] I. Agi and L. Gong. An empirical study of secure MPEG video transmissions. In *ISOC Symposium on Network and Distributed Systems Security*, pages 137–144, San Diego, California, 1996.

[5] A. Alattar G. Al-Regib. Evaluation of selective encryption techniques for secure transmission of MPEG-compressed bit-streams. In *Proceedings of the IEEE International Symposium on Circuits and Systems*, pages IV–340–IV–343, 1999.

[6] A. M. Alattar, G. I. Al-Regib, and S. A. Al-Semari. Improved selective encryption techniques for secure transmission of MPEG video bit-streams. In *Proceedings of the IEEE International Conference on Image Processing (ICIP'99)*, volume 4, pages 256–260, Kobe, Japan, October 1999. IEEE Signal Processing Society.

[7] M. Antonini, M. Barlaud, P. Mathieu, and I. Daubechies. Image coding using wavelet transform. *IEEE Transactions on Image Processing*, 1(2):205–220, 1992.

[8] S. Appadwedula, M. Goel, N. R. Shanbhag, D. L. Jones, and K. Ramchandran. Total system energy minimization for wireless image transmission. *Journal of VLSI Signal Processing*, 27:99–117, 2001.

[9] D. Atkins, W. Stallings, and P. Zimmermann. RFC 1991: PGP message exchange formats, August 1996. available online from ftp://ftp.rfc-editor.org/in-notes/rfc1991.txt.

[10] A. Averbuch, D. Lazar, and M. Israeli. Image compression using wavelet transform and multiresolution decomposition. *IEEE Trans. on Image Process.*, 5(1):4–15, 1996.

[11] M.F. Barnsley and L.P. Hurd. *Fractal Image Compression.* AK Peters, Ltd, Wellesley, Massachusetts, 1993.

[12] Simon Bewick. Descrambling DVB data according to ETSI common scrambling standard. European Patent GB2322995, 1998-09-09. available online from http://www.european-patent-office.org/.

[13] Simon Bewick. Digital video broadcasting. European Patent GB2322994, 2002-06-18. available online from http://www.european-patent-office.org/.

[14] B. Bhargava, C. Shi, and Y. Wang. MPEG video encryption algorithms. *Multimedia Tools and Applications*, 24(1):57–79, 2004.

[15] S. Blake-Wilson, M. Nystrom, D. Hopwood, J. Mikkelsen, and T. Wright. RFC 3546: Transport layer security (TLS) extensions, June 2003. available online from ftp://ftp.rfc-editor.org/in-notes/rfc3546.txt.

[16] Jeffrey A. Bloom, Ingemar J. Cox, Ton Kalker, Jean-Paul Linnartz, Matthew L. Miller, and B. Traw. Copy protection for DVD video. *Proceedings of the IEEE Special issue on Identification and Protection of Multimedia Information*, 87(7):1267–1276, 1999.

[17] Y. Bodo, N. Laurent, and J.-L. Degelay. A scrambling method based on disturbance of motion vector. In *Proceedings of ACM Multimedia 2002*, pages 89–90, Juan Le Pins, France, December 2003.

[18] Jason But. Limitations of existing MPEG-1 ciphers for streaming video. Technical Report CAIA 040429A, Swinburne University, Australia, April 2004.

[19] J. Callas, L. Donnerhacke, H. Finney, and R. Thayer. RFC 2440: OpenPGP message format, November 1998. available online from ftp://ftp.rfc-editor.org/in-notes/rfc2440.txt.

[20] T. S. Chen, C. C. Chang, and M. S. Hwang. Virtual image cryptosystem based upon vector quantization. *IEEE Transactions on Image Processing*, 7(10):1485–1488, October 1998.

[21] H. Cheng and X. Li. On the application of image decomposition to image compression and encryption. In P. Horster, editor, *Communications and Multimedia Security II, IFIP TC6/TC11 Second Joint Working Conference on Communications and Multimedia Security, CMS '96*, pages 116–127, Essen, Germany, September 1996. Chapman & Hall.

[22] H. Cheng and X. Li. Partial encryption of compressed images and videos. *IEEE Transactions on Signal Processing*, 48(8):2439–2451, 2000.

[23] Charilaos Christopoulos, Athanassios N. Skodras, and Touradj Ebrahimi. The JPEG2000 still image coding system: an overwiew. *IEEE Transactions on Consumer Electronics*, 46(4):1103–1127, November 2000.

[24] T.-J. Chuang and J.-C. Lin. New approach to image encryption. *Journal of Electronic Imaging*, 7(2):350–356, 1998.

[25] C.K. Chui, editor. *Wavelets: A Tutorial in Theory and Applications.* Academic Press, San Diego, 1992.

[26] P.C. Cosman, R.M. Gray, and M. Vetterli. Vector quantization of image subbands: A review. *IEEE Transactions on Image Processing*, 5(2):202–225, 1996.

[27] J. Daemen and V. Rijmen. The block cipher rijndael. In J.-J. Quisquater and B. Schneier, editors, *Smart Card Research and Applications*, volume 1820 of *LNCS*, pages 288–296. Springer Verlag, 2000.

[28] J. Daemen and V. Rijmen. Rijndael, the advanced encryption standard. *Dr. Dobb's Journal*, 26(3):137–139, March 2001.

[29] J. Daemen and V. Rijmen. *The Design of Rijndael: AES — The Advanced Encryption Standard*. Springer Verlag, 2002.

[30] G. Davis. Self-quantized wavelet subtrees: A wavelet-based theory for fractal image compression. In J.A. Storer and M.A. Cohn, editors, *Proceedings Data Compression Conference (DCC'95)*, pages 232–241. IEEE Computer Society Press, March 1995.

[31] Philippe Desarte, Benoit M. Macq, and Dirk T. M. Slock. Signal-adapted multiresolution transform for image coding. *IEEE Transactions on Information Theory*, 38(2):897–904, March 1992.

[32] T. Dierks and C. Allen. RFC 2246: The TLS protocol version 1.0, January 1999. available online from ftp://ftp.rfc-editor.org/in-notes/rfc2246.txt.

[33] W. M. Dietl and A. Uhl. Robustness against unauthorized watermark removal attacks via key-dependent wavelet packet subband structures. In *Proceedings of the IEEE International Conference on Multimedia and Expo, ICME '04*, Taipei, Taiwan, June 2004.

[34] Werner Dietl, Peter Meerwald, and Andreas Uhl. Protection of wavelet-based watermarking systems using filter parametrization. *Signal Processing (Special Issue on Security of Data Hiding Technologies)*, 83:2095–2116, 2003.

[35] Jana Dittmann and Ralf Steinmetz. Enabling technology for the trading of MPEG-encoded video. In *Information Security and Privacy: Second Australasian Conference, ACISP '97*, volume 1270, pages 314–324, July 1997.

[36] Jana Dittmann and Ralf Steinmetz. A technical approach to the transparent encryption of MPEG-2 video. In S. K. Katsikas, editor, *Communications and Multimedia Security, IFIP TC6/TC11 Third Joint Working Conference, CMS '97*, pages 215–226, Athens, Greece, September 1997. Chapman and Hall.

[37] Igor Djurovic, Srdjan Stankovic, and Ioannis Pitas. Digital watermarking in the fractional fourier transformation domain. *Journal of Network and Computer Applications*, 24:167–173, 2001.

[38] Marc Van Droogenbroeck. Partial encryption of images for real-time applications. In *Proceedings of the 4th 2004 Benelux Signal Processing Symposium*, pages 11–15, Hilvarenbeek, The Netherlands, April 2004.

[39] Marc Van Droogenbroeck and Raphaël Benedett. Techniques for a selective encryption of uncompressed and compressed images. In *Proceedings of ACIVS (Advanced Concepts for Intelligent Vision Systems)*, pages 90–97, Ghent University, Belgium, September 2002.

[40]  T. Ebrahimi and F. Pereira. *The MPEG-4 book.* Pearson Education, 2002.

[41]  Ahmet Eskicioglu and Edward J. Delp. An integrated approach to encrypting scalable video. In *Proceedings of the IEEE International Conference on Multimedia and Expo, ICME '02,* Laussanne, Switzerland, August 2002.

[42]  Ahmet M. Eskicioglu and Edward J. Delp. An overview of multimedia content protection in consumer electronics devices. *Signal Processing: Image Communication,* 16(7):681–699, 2001.

[43]  Ahmet M. Eskicioglu, Scott Dexter, and Edward J. Delp. Protection of multicast scalable video by secret sharing: Simulation results. In *Proceedings of SPIE Security and Watermarking of Multimedia Contents V,* volume 5020, Santa Clara, CA, USA, January 2003. SPIE.

[44]  Ahmet M. Eskicioglu, John Town, and Edward J. Delp. Security of digital entertainment content from creation to consumption. *Signal Processing: Image Communication, Special Issue on Image Security,* 18(4):237–262, April 2003. invited paper.

[45]  ETSI. Guideline for use of DVB standards ("cookbook"), November 1998. URL: http://portal.etsi.org/broadcast/cookbook.asp, 2004-07-06.

[46]  Mark M. Fisch, Herbert Stögner, and Andreas Uhl. Layered encryption techniques for DCT-coded visual data. In *Proceedings of the European Signal Processing Conference, EUSIPCO '04,* Vienna, Austria, September 2004.

[47]  Y. Fisher, editor. *Fractal Image Compression: Theory and Application.* Springer-Verlag, New York, 1995.

[48]  Bubi G. Flepp-Stars, Herbert Stögner, and Andreas Uhl. Confidential transmission of lossless visual data: Experimental modelling and optimization. In A. Lioy and D. Mazzocchi, editors, *Communications and Multimedia Security. Proceedings of the IFIP TC6/TC11 Sixth Joint Working Conference on Communications and Multimedia Security, CMS '03,* volume 2828 of *Lecture Notes on Computer Science,* pages 252 – 263, Turin, Italy, October 2003. Springer-Verlag.

[49]  Electronic Frontier Foundation. *Cracking DES.* O'Reilly, July 1998.

[50]  Jiri Fridrich. Image encryption based on chaotic maps. In *Proceedings of the IEEE Conference on Systems, Man, and Cybernetics,* pages 1105–1110, 1997.

[51]  Jiri Fridrich. Symmetric ciphers based on two-dimensional chaotic maps. *International Journal on Bifurcation and Chaos,* 8(6), June 1998.

[52]  J. Froment and S. Mallat. Second generation compact image coding. In [25], pages 655–678. Academic Press, 1992.

[53]  B. Furht, J. Greenberg, and R. Westwater. *Motion estimation algorithms for video compression.* Kluwer Academic Publishers Group, Norwell, MA, USA, and Dordrecht, The Netherlands, 1997.

[54]  B. Furht and D. Kirovski, editors. *Multimedia Security Handbook.* CRC Press, Boca Raton, Florida, 2004.

[55] C. Griwotz. Video protection by partial content corruption. In *Multimedia and Security Workshop at the 6th ACM International Multimedia Conference*, pages 37–39, Bristol, England, 1998.

[56] C. Griwotz, O. Merkel, J. Dittmann, and R. Steinmetz. Protecting VOD the easier way. In *Proceedings of the 6th ACM Multimedia Conference*, pages 21–28, Bristol, England, 1998.

[57] Raphaël Grosbois, Pierre Gerbelot, and Touradj Ebrahimi. Authentication and access control in the JPEG 2000 compressed domain. In A.G. Tescher, editor, *Applications of Digital Image Processing XXIV*, volume 4472 of *Proceedings of SPIE*, pages 95–104, San Diego, CA, USA, July 2001.

[58] J. Guimaraes, J. Boucqueau, and B. Macq. OKAPI: a kernel for access control to multimedia services based on TTPs. In *Proceedings of the 1996 ECMAST European Conference on Multimedia Applications, Services and Techniques*, pages 783–798, 1996.

[59] F. Hartenstein. Parametrization of discrete finite biorthogonal wavelets with linear phase. In *Proceedings of the 1997 International Conference on Acoustics, Speech and Signal Processing (ICASSP'97)*, April 1997.

[60] B.G. Haskell, A. Puri, and A.N. Netravali. *Digital video: an introduction to MPEG-2*. Digital Multimedia Standards Series. Chapman & Hall, 1997.

[61] G. Held. *Data and image compression: tools and techniques*. John Wiley & Sons, 4 edition, 1996.

[62] M.L. Hilton, B.D. Jawerth, and A. Sengupta. Compressing still and moving images with wavelets. *Multimedia Systems*, 3(2), 1995.

[63] R. Housley. RFC 3686: Using advanced encryption standard (AES) counter mode with ipsec encapsulating security payload (ESP), January 2004. available online from `ftp://ftp.rfc-editor.org/in-notes/rfc3686.txt`.

[64] B. Jawerth and W. Sweldens. Biorthogonal smooth local trigonometric bases. *J. Fourier Anal. Appl.*, 2(2):109–133, 1995.

[65] D. Kahn. *The Codebreakers*. Simon & Schuster Inc., revised edition, October 1997.

[66] Chandrapal Kailasanathan. Compression performance of JPEG encryption scheme. In *Proceedings of the 14th International IEEE Conference on Digital Signal Processing, DSP '02*, July 2002.

[67] M. S. Kankanhalli and K. F. Hau. Watermarking of electronic text documents. *Electronic Commerce Research*, 2(1):169–187, 2002.

[68] Stefan Katzenbeisser and Fabien A. P. Petitcolas. *Information Hiding Techniques for Steganography and Digital Watermarking*. Artech House, December 1999.

[69] Jaroslav Kautsky and Radka Turcajova. Pollen product factorization and construction of higher multiplicity wavelets. *Linear Algebra and its Applications*, 222:241–260, 1995.

[70] Auguste Kerckhoff. La cryptographie militaire. *Journal des sciences militaires*, 9:5–38, January 1883.

[71] Jeong Hyun Kim, Seong Oun Hwang, Ki Song Yoon, and Chang Soon Park. MPEG-21 IPMP. In *First International Conference on Information Technology and Applications — ICITA 2002*, Bathurst, Australia, November 2002.

[72] H. Kiya, D. Imaizumi, and O. Watanabe. Partial-scrambling of image encoded using JPEG2000 without generating marker codes. In *Proceedings of the IEEE International Conference on Image Processing (ICIP'03)*, volume III, pages 205–208, Barcelona, Spain, September 2003.

[73] T. Köckerbauer, M. Kumar, and A. Uhl. Lightweight JPEG 2000 confidentiality for mobile environments. In *Proceedings of the IEEE International Conference on Multimedia and Expo, ICME '04*, Taipei, Taiwan, June 2004.

[74] T. Kunkelmann. *Sicherheit für Videodaten*. Vieweg Verlag, 1998.

[75] T. Kunkelmann and U. Horn. Partial video encryption based on scalable coding. In $5^{\text{th}}$ *International Workshop on Systems, Signals and Image Processing (IWSSIP'98)*, pages 215–218, Zagreb, Croatia, 1998.

[76] Thomas Kunkelmann. Applying encryption to video communication. In *Proceedings of the Multimedia and Security Workshop at ACM Multimedia '98*, pages 41–47, Bristol, England, September 1998.

[77] Thomas Kunkelmann and Rolf Reinema. A scalable security architecture for multimedia communication standards. In *Proceedings of the IEEE International Conference on Multimedia Computing and Systems (ICMCS'97)*, pages 660–661, Ottawa, Canada, June 1997.

[78] R. Kutil. A significance map based adaptive wavelet zerotree codec (SMAWZ). In S. Panchanathan, V. Bove, and S.I. Sudharsanan, editors, *Media Processors 2002*, volume 4674 of *SPIE Proceedings*, pages 61–71, January 2002.

[79] T. Lan and A. Tewfik. Adaptive low power multimedia wireless communications. In *Proceedings of the Conference on Information Sciences and Systems*, pages 377–382, 1997.

[80] G. Leduc, O. Bonaventure, E. Koerner, L. Leonard, C. Pecheur, and D. Zanetti. Specification and verification of a TTP protocol for the conditional access to services. In *Proceedings of the 12th J.Cartier Workshop on Formal Methods and their applications: Telecommunications, VLSI and Real-Time Computerised Control Systems*, 1996.

[81] A.S. Lewis and G. Knowles. Image compression using the 2-D wavelet transform. *IEEE Trans. on Image Process.*, 1(2):244–250, April 1992.

[82] X. Li, J. Knipe, and H. Cheng. Image compression and encryption using tree structure. *Pattern Recognition Letters*, 18:1253–1259, 1997.

[83] Yongcheng Li, Zhigang Chen, See-Mong Tan, and Roy H. Campbell. Security enhanced MPEG player. In *Proceedings of IEEE First International Workshop on Multimedia Software Development (MMSD'96)*, pages 169–175, Berlin, Germany, 1996.

[84] T.D. Lookabaugh and D.C. Sicker. Selective encryption for consumer applications. *IEEE Communications Magazine*, 42(5):124–129, 2004.

[85] T.D. Lookabaugh, D.C. Sicker, D.M. Keaton, W.Y. Guo, and I. Vedula. Security analysis of selectiveley encrypted MPEG-2 streams. In *Multimedia Systems and Applications VI*, volume 5241 of *Proceedings of SPIE*, pages 10–21, September 2003.

[86] J. Lu, V.R. Algazi, and R.R. Estes. Comparative study of wavelet image coders. *Optical Engineering*, 35(9):2605–2619, 1996.

[87] Xiliang Lu and Ahmet M. Eskicioglu. Selective encryption of multimedia content in distribution networks: Challenges and new directions. In *Proceedings of the IASTED International Conference on on Communications, Internet and Information Technology (CIIT 2003)*, Scottsdale, AZ, USA, November 2003.

[88] B. Macq and J.Y. Mertes. Optimization of linear multiresolution transforms for scene adaptive coding. *IEEE Trans. on Signal Process.*, 41(12):3568–3572, 1993.

[89] B. Macq and J.J. Quisquater. Digital images multiresolution encryption. *The Journal of the Interactive Multimedia Association Intellectual Property Project*, 1(1):179–206, January 1994.

[90] Benoit M. Macq and Jean-Jacques Quisquater. Cryptology for digital TV broadcasting. *Proceedings of the IEEE*, 83(6):944–957, June 1995.

[91] S. Mallat. A theory for multiresolution signal decomposition: The wavelet representation. *IEEE Trans. on Patt. Anal. and Mach. Intell.*, 11(7):674–693, July 1989.

[92] S. Maslakovic, I. R. Linscott, M. Oslick, and J. D. Twicken. A library-based approach to design of smooth orthonormal wavelets. In *Proceedings of the IEEE Digital Signal Processing Workshop, DSP '98*, Bryce Canyon, USA, August 1998.

[93] S. Maslakovic, I. R. Linscott, M. Oslick, and J. D. Twicken. Smooth orthonormal wavelet libraries: design and application. In *Proceedings of the 1998 International Conference on Acoustics, Speech and Signal Processing (ICASSP'98)*, pages 1793–1796, Seattle, WA, USA, May 1998.

[94] Peter Meerwald, Roland Norcen, and Andreas Uhl. Cache issues with JPEG2000 wavelet lifting. In C.-C. Jay Kuo, editor, *Visual Communications and Image Processing 2002 (VCIP'02)*, volume 4671 of *SPIE Proceedings*, pages 626–634, San Jose, CA, USA, January 2002. SPIE.

[95] Peter Meerwald, Roland Norcen, and Andreas Uhl. Parallel JPEG2000 image coding on multiprocessors. In *Proceedings of the International Parallel & Distributed Processing Symposium 2002 (IPDPS'02)*, page 2, Fort Lauderdale, FL, USA, April 2002. IEEE Computer Society Press.

[96] A.J. Menezes, P.v. Oorschot, and S.A. Vanston. *Handbook of Applied Cryptography*. CRC Press, October 1996.

[97] J. Meyer and F. Gadegast. Securitymechanisms for mulimedia-data with the example MPEG-I-video, 1995. unpublished, available at http://www.gadegast.de/frank/doc/secmeng.pdf.

[98] Ji Ming and SM Shen. MPEG IPMP extensions overview. ISO/IEC JTC1/SC29/WG11 N6338, March 2004.

[99] J.L. Mitchell et al. *MPEG video compression standard.* Digital Multimedia Standards Series. Chapman & Hall, 1997.

[100] Klara Nahrstedt and Lintian Qiao. Is MPEG Encryption by Using Random List Instead of ZigZag Order Secure ? In *Proceedings of Int. Sym. Consumer Electronics (ISCE97)*, pages 226–229, 1997.

[101] National Institute of Standards and Technology. FIPS-46-3 - data encryption standard (DES), July 1977.

[102] National Institute of Standards and Technology. FIPS-197 - advanced encryption standard (AES), November 2001.

[103] National Institute of Standards and Technology. Announcing proposed withdrawal of federal information processing standard (FIPS) for the data encryption standard (DES) and request for comments. *Federal Register*, 69(142):44509–44510, 2004-07-26. available online from http://www.access.gpo.gov/su_docs/fedreg/a040726c.html.

[104] R. Norcen, M. Podesser, A. Pommer, H.-P. Schmidt, and A. Uhl. Confidential storage and transmission of medical image data. *Computers in Biology and Medicine*, 33(3):277 – 292, 2003.

[105] R. Norcen and A. Uhl. Encryption of wavelet-coded imagery using random permutations. In *Proceedings of the IEEE International Conference on Image Processing (ICIP'04)*, Singapure, October 2004. IEEE Signal Processing Society.

[106] Roland Norcen and Andreas Uhl. Selective encryption of the JPEG2000 bitstream. In A. Lioy and D. Mazzocchi, editors, *Communications and Multimedia Security. Proceedings of the IFIP TC6/TC11 Sixth Joint Working Conference on Communications and Multimedia Security, CMS '03*, volume 2828 of *Lecture Notes on Computer Science*, pages 194 – 204, Turin, Italy, October 2003. Springer-Verlag.

[107] J.E. Odegard and C.S.Burrus. Smooth biorthogonal wavelets for applications in image compression. In *IEEE DSP Workshop, Loen, Norway*, September 1996.

[108] M. Oslick, I. R. Linscott, S. Maslakovic, and J. D. Twicken. A general aproach to the generation of biorthogonal bases of compactly-supported wavelets. In *Proceedings of the 1998 International Conference on Acoustics, Speech and Signal Processing (ICASSP'98)*, Seattle, WA, USA, May 1998.

[109] Cheng Peng, Robert Deng, Yongdong Wu, and Weizhong Shao. A flexible and scalable authentication scheme for JPEG2000 codestreams. In *Proceedings of ACM Multimedia 2003*, pages 433–441, San Francisco, CA, USA, November 2003.

[110] W.B. Pennebaker and J.L. Mitchell. *JPEG – Still image compression standard.* Van Nostrand Reinhold, New York, 1993.

[111] S.-M. Phoong, C.W. Kim, P.P. Vaidyanathan, and R. Ansari. A new class of twochannel biorthogonal filter banks and wavelet bases. *IEEE Transactions on Signal Processing*, 43(3), March 1995.

[112] M. Podesser, H.-P. Schmidt, and A. Uhl. Selective bitplane encryption for secure transmission of image data in mobile environments. In *CD-ROM Proceedings of the 5th*

*IEEE Nordic Signal Processing Symposium (NORSIG 2002)*, Tromso-Trondheim, Norway, October 2002. IEEE Norway Section. file cr1037.pdf.

[113] A. Pommer and A. Uhl. Wavelet packet methods for multimedia compression and encryption. In *Proceedings of the 2001 IEEE Pacific Rim Conference on Communications, Computers and Signal Processing*, pages 1–4, Victoria, Canada, August 2001. IEEE Signal Processing Society.

[114] A. Pommer and A. Uhl. Application scenarios for selective encryption of visual data. In J. Dittmann, J. Fridrich, and P. Wohlmacher, editors, *Multimedia and Security Workshop, ACM Multimedia*, pages 71–74, Juan-les-Pins, France, December 2002.

[115] A. Pommer and A. Uhl. Selective encryption of wavelet packet subband structures for obscured transmission of visual data. In *Proceedings of the 3rd IEEE Benelux Signal Processing Symposium (SPS 2002)*, pages 25–28, Leuven, Belgium, March 2002. IEEE Benelux Signal Processing Chapter.

[116] A. Pommer and A. Uhl. Selective encryption of wavelet packet subband structures for secure transmission of visual data. In J. Dittmann, J. Fridrich, and P. Wohlmacher, editors, *Multimedia and Security Workshop, ACM Multimedia*, pages 67–70, Juan-les-Pins, France, December 2002.

[117] A. Pommer and A. Uhl. Selective encryption of wavelet-packet encoded image data — efficiency and security. *ACM Multimedia Systems (Special issue on Multimedia Security)*, 9(3):279–287, 2003.

[118] A. Pommer and A. Uhl. Are parameterised biorthogonal wavelet filters suited (better) for selective encryption? In J. Dittmann and J. Fridrich, editors, *ACM Multimedia and Security Workshop*, Magdeburg, Germany, September 2004.

[119] Lintian Qiao and Klara Nahrstedt. A new algorithm for MPEG video encryption. In *Proceedings of the International Conference on Imaging Science, Systems, and Technology, CISST '97*, pages 21–29, Las Vegas, NV, USA, June 1997.

[120] Lintian Qiao and Klara Nahrstedt. Comparison of MPEG encryption algorithms. *International Journal on Computers and Graphics (Special Issue on Data Security in Image Communication and Networks)*, 22(3):437–444, 1998.

[121] Eric Rescorla. *SSL and TLS — Designing and Building Secure Systems*. Addison-Wesley, second edition, March 2001.

[122] Howard L. Resnikoff, Jun Tian, and Raymond O. Wells. Biorthogonal wavelet space: parametrization and factorization. *SIAM Journal on Mathematical Analysis*, August 1999.

[123] Mara Rhepp, Herbert Stögner, and Andreas Uhl. Comparison of JPEG and JPEG 2000 in low-power confidential image transmission. In *Proceedings of the European Signal Processing Conference, EUSIPCO '04*, Vienna, Austria, September 2004.

[124] I.E.G. Richardson. *H.264 and MPEG-4 video compression: video coding for next generation multimedia*. Wiley & Sons, 2003.

[125] Stephane Roche, Jean-Luc Dugelay, and R. Molva. Multi-resolution access control algorithm based on fractal coding. In *Proceedings of the IEEE International Conference on Image Processing (ICIP'96)*, pages 235–238, Lausanne, Switzerland, September 1996. IEEE Signal Processing Society.

[126] Amir Said and William A. Pearlman. A new, fast, and efficient image codec based on set partitioning in hierarchical trees. *IEEE Transactions on Circuits and Systems for Video Technology*, 6(3):243–249, June 1996.

[127] Diego Santa-Cruz and Touradj Ebrahimi. A study of JPEG 2000 still image coding versus other standards. In *Proceedings of the 10th European Signal Processing Conference, EUSIPCO '00*, Tampere, Finland, September 2000.

[128] J. Scharinger. Fast encryption of image data using chaotic Kolmogorov flows. *Journal of Electorinic Imaging*, 7(2):318–325, 1998.

[129] Josef Scharinger. Robust watermark generation for multimedia copyright protection. In *Proceedings of IWSSIP '99*, pages 177–180, Bratislava, Slovakia, 1999.

[130] J. Schneid and S. Pittner. On the parametrization of the coefficients of dilation equations for compactly supported wavelets. *Computing*, 51:165–173, May 1993.

[131] B. Schneier. *Applied cryptography (2nd edition): protocols, algorithms and source code in C*. Wiley Publishers, 1996.

[132] B. Schneier. *Secret and Lies*. John Wiley & Sons, first edition, August 2000.

[133] WG1, SC29 Secretariat. Resolutions of the $32^{nd}$ ISO/IEC JTC 1/SC 29/WG1 meeting, Madrid, Spain, 2004-03-29 to 2004-04-02. URL: http://www.itscj.ipsj.or.jp/sc29/open/29view/29n59691.pdf, 2004-07-14.

[134] Yong-Seok Seo, Min-Su Kim, Ha-Joong Park, Ho-Youl Jung, Hyun-Yeol Chung, Young Huh, and Jae-Duck Lee. A secure watermarking for JPEG-2000. In *Proceedings of the IEEE International Conference on Image Processing (ICIP'01)*, Thessaloniki, Greece, October 2001.

[135] Jerome M. Shapiro. Embedded image coding using zerotrees of wavelet coefficients. *IEEE Trans. on Signal Process.*, 41(12):3445–3462, December 1993.

[136] C. Shi and B. Bhargava. An efficent MPEG video encryption algorithm. In *Proceedings of the 17th IEEE Symposium on Reliable Distributed Systems*, pages 381–386, West Lafayette, Indiana, USA, 1998.

[137] C. Shi and B. Bhargava. A fast MPEG video encryption algorithm. In *Proceedings of the Sixth ACM International Multimedia Conference*, pages 81–88, Bristol, UK, September 1998.

[138] C. Shi and B. Bhargava. Light-weight MPEG video encryption algorithm. In *Proceedings of the International Conference on Multimedia (Multimedia98 Shaping the Future)*, pages 55–61, New Delhi, India, January 1998.

[139] Changgui Shi, Sheng-Yih Wang, and Bharat Bhargava. MPEG video encryption in real-time using secret key cryptography. In *Proceedings of the International Conference on*

*Parallel and Distributed Processing Techniques and Applications (PDPTA'99)*, pages 2822–2829, Las Vegas, Nevada, 1999.

[140] S.U. Shin, K.S. Sim, and K.H. Rhee. A secrecy scheme for MPEG video data using the joint of compression and encryption. In *Proceedings of the 1999 Information Security Workshop (ISW'99)*, volume 1729 of *Lecture Notes on Computer Science*, pages 191–201, Kuala Lumpur, November 1999. Springer-Verlag.

[141] D. Simitopoulos, N. Zissis, P. Georgiadis, V. Emmanouilidis, and M.G. Strintzis. Encryption and watermarking for the secure distribution of copyrighted MPEG video on DVD. *ACM Multimedia Systems (Special issue on Multimedia Security)*, 9(3):217–227, 2003.

[142] B. Simon. Image coding using overlapping fractal transform in the wavelet domain. In *Proceedings of the IEEE International Conference on Image Processing (ICIP'96)*, volume I, pages 177–180, Lausanne, September 1996. IEEE Signal Processing Society.

[143] Champskud J. Skrepth and Andreas Uhl. Selective encryption of visual data: Classification of application scenarios and comparison of techniques for lossless environments. In B. Jerman-Blazic and T. Klobucar, editors, *Advanced Communications and Multimedia Security, IFIP TC6/TC11 Sixth Joint Working Conference on Communications and Multimedia Security, CMS '02*, pages 213 – 226, Portoroz, Slovenia, September 2002. Kluver Academic Publishing.

[144] L. T. Smit, G. J. M. Smit, and J. L. Hurink. Energy-efficient wireless communication for mobile multimedia terminals. In *Proceedings of the International Conference on Advances in Mobile Multimedia (MoMM2003)*, pages 115–124. Austrian Computer Society, 2003.

[145] G. Spanos and T. Maples. Performance study of a selective encryption scheme for the security of networked real-time video. In *Proceedings of the 4th International Conference on Computer Communications and Networks (ICCCN'95)*, Las Vegas, NV, 1995.

[146] Francois-Xavier Standaert, Gilles Piret, and Jean-Jacques Quisquater. Cryptanalysis of block ciphers: A survey. Technical Report CG–2003/2, Crypto Group, Catholic University of Louvain (UCL), Belgium, 2003.

[147] F.A. Stevenson. Cryptanalysis of contents scrambling system, November 1999. published online on many places, e.g. here: http://www.insecure.org/news/cryptanalysis_of_contents_scrambling_system.htm.

[148] N. Taesombut, R. Huang, and V.P. Rangan. A secure multimedia system in emerging wireless home networks. In A. Lioy and D. Mazzocchi, editors, *Communications and Multimedia Security. Proceedings of the IFIP TC6/TC11 Sixth Joint Working Conference on Communications and Multimedia Security, CMS '03*, volume 2828 of *Lecture Notes on Computer Science*, pages 76–88, Turin, Italy, October 2003. Springer-Verlag.

[149] L. Tang. Methods for encrypting and decrypting MPEG video data efficiently. In *Proceedings of the ACM Multimedia 1996*, pages 219–229, Boston, USA, November 1996.

[150] C. Taswell and K.C. McGill. Wavelet transform algorithms for finite-duration discrete-time signals. *ACM Transactions on Mathematical Software*, 20(3):398–412, September 1994.

[151]  D. Taubman.  High performance scalable image compression with EBCOT. *IEEE Transactions on Image Processing*, 9(7):1158 – 1170, 2000.

[152]  D. Taubman and M.W. Marcellin.  *JPEG2000 — Image Compression Fundamentals, Standards and Practice*. Kluwer Academic Publishers, 2002.

[153]  A.M. Tekalp. *Digital Video Processing*. Prentice Hall, One Lake Street, Upper Saddle River, NJ 07458, USA, 1995.

[154]  P.N. Topiwala, editor. *Wavelet Image and Video Compression*. Kluwer Academic Publishers Group, Boston, 1998.

[155]  Ali Saman Tosun and Wu chi Feng.  Efficient multi-layer coding and encryption of MPEG video streams. In *Proceedings of the IEEE International Conference on Multimedia and Expo, ICME '00*, pages 119–122, New York, USA, August 2000.

[156]  Ali Saman Tosun and Wu chi Feng.  Lightweight security mechanisms for wireless video transmission. In *Proceedings of the IEEE International Conference on Information Technology: Coding and Computing (ITCC '01)*, pages 157–161, Las Vegas, NV, USA, April 2001.

[157]  Ali Saman Tosun and Wu chi Feng.  On error preserving encryption algorithms for wireless video transmission. In *Proceedings of the ninth ACM Multimedia Conference 2001*, pages 302–307, Ottawa, Canada, October 2001.

[158]  T. Uehara and R. Safavi-Naini.  Chosen DCT coefficients attack on MPEG encryption schemes. In *Proceedings of the 2000 IEEE Pacific Rim Conference on Multimedia*, pages 316–319, Sydney, December 2000. IEEE Signal Processing Society.

[159]  T. Uehara, R. Safavi-Naini, and P. Ogunbona.  Securing wavelet compression with random permutations. In *Proceedings of the 2000 IEEE Pacific Rim Conference on Multimedia*, pages 332–335, Sydney, December 2000. IEEE Signal Processing Society.

[160]  A. Uhl.  Image compression using non-stationary and inhomogeneous multiresolution analyses. *Image and Vision Computing*, 14(5):365–371, 1996.

[161]  A. Uhl.  Generalized wavelet decompositions in image compression: arbitrary subbands and parallel algorithms. *Optical Engineering*, 36(5):1480–1487, 1997.

[162]  G. Unnikrishnan and Kehar Singh.  Double random fractional fourier-domain encoding for optical security. *Optical Engineering*, 39(11):2853–2859, November 2000.

[163]  Chitra Venkatramani, Peter Westerink, Olivier Verscheure, and Pascal Frossard.  Securing media for adaptive streaming. In *Proceedings of the 11th ACM Multimedia 2003 Conference*, pages 307–310, Berkeley, CA, USA, 2003.

[164]  John D. Villasenor, B. Belzer, and J. Liao.  Wavelet filter evaluation for image compression. *IEEE Transactions on Image Processing*, 4(8):1053–1060, August 1995.

[165]  K. Violka and S. Porteck.  Wieder alles umsonst? Angriff auf neue Premiere-Verschlüsselung (German). *CT*, 24, 2003.

[166]  L. Vorwerk, T. Engel, and C. Meinel.  A proposal for a combination of compression and encryption. In *Visual Communications and Image Processing 2000*, volume 4067 of *Proceedings of SPIE*, pages 694–702, Perth, Australia, June 2000.

[167] George Voyatzis and Ioannis Pitas. Chaotic mixing of digital images and applications to watermarking. In *European Conference on Multimedia Applications, Services and Techniques, ECMAST '96*, volume 2, pages 687–695, Louvain-la-Neuve, Belgium, May 1996.

[168] David Wagner. The boomerang attack. In *Proceedings of FSE 1999*, volume 1636 of *Lecture Notes in Computer Science*, pages 156–170. Springer Verlag, 1999.

[169] G.K. Wallace. The JPEG still picture compression standard. *Communications of the ACM*, 34(4):30–44, 1991.

[170] S.J. Wee and J.G. Apostolopoulos. Secure scalable streaming enabling transcoding without decryption. In *Proceedings of the IEEE International Conference on Image Processing (ICIP'01)*, Thessaloniki, Greece, October 2001.

[171] S.J. Wee and J.G. Apostolopoulos. Secure scalable video streaming for wireless networks. In *Proceedings of the 2001 International Conference on Acoustics, Speech and Signal Processing (ICASSP 2001)*, Salt Lake City, Utah, USA, April 2001. invited paper.

[172] S.J. Wee and J.G. Apostolopoulos. Secure scalable streaming and secure transcoding with JPEG2000. In *Proceedings of the IEEE International Conference on Image Processing (ICIP'03)*, volume I, pages 547–551, Barcelona, Spain, September 2003.

[173] Jiangtao Wen, Mike Severa, Wenjun Zeng, Max Luttrell, and Weiyin Jin. A format-compliant configurable encryption framework for access control of multimedia. In *Proceedings of the IEEE Workshop on Multimedia Signal Processing, MMSP '01*, pages 435–440, Cannes, France, October 2001.

[174] Jiangtao Wen, Mike Severa, Wenjun Zeng, Max Luttrell, and Weiyin Jin. A format-compliant configurable encryption framework for access control of video. *IEEE Transactions on Circuits and Systems for Video Technology*, 12(6):545–557, June 2002.

[175] M.V. Wickerhauser. *Adapted wavelet analysis from theory to software*. A.K. Peters, Wellesley, Mass., 1994.

[176] S. Wong, L. Zaremba, D. Gooden, and H.K. Huang. Radiologic image compression – a review. *Proceedings of the IEEE*, 83(2):194–219, 1995.

[177] Chung-Ping Wu and C.-C. Jay Kuo. Fast encryption methods for audiovisual data confidentiality. In *SPIE Photonics East - Symposium on Voice, Video, and Data Communications*, volume 4209, pages 284–295, Boston, MA, USA, November 2000.

[178] Chung-Ping Wu and C.-C. Jay Kuo. Efficient multimedia encryption via entropy codec design. In *Proceedings of SPIE, Security and Watermarking of Multimedia Contents III*, volume 4314, San Jose, CA, USA, January 2001.

[179] Tsung-Li Wu and S. Felix Wu. Selective encryption and watermarking of MPEG video (extended abstract). In Hamid R. Arabnia, editor, *Proceedings of the International Conference on Image Science, Systems, and Technology, CISST '97*, Las Vegas, USA, February 1997.

[180] Yongdong Wu and Robert H. Deng. Compliant encryption of JPEG2000 codestreams. In *Proceedings of the IEEE International Conference on Image Processing (ICIP'04)*, Singapure, October 2004. IEEE Signal Processing Society.

[181] Yongdong Wu and Robert H. Deng. Progressive protection of JPEG2000 codestreams. In *Proceedings of the IEEE International Conference on Image Processing (ICIP'04)*, Singapure, October 2004. IEEE Signal Processing Society.

[182] C. Yuan, B. B. Zhu, M. Su, Y. Wang, S. Li, and Y. Zhong. Layered access control for MPEG-4 FGS. In *Proceedings of the IEEE International Conference on Image Processing (ICIP'03)*, Barcelona, Spain, September 2003.

[183] C. Yuan, B. B. Zhu, Y. Wang, S. Li, and Y. Zhong. Efficient and fully scalable encryption for MPEG-4 FGS. In *IEEE International Symposium on Circuits and Systems (ISCAS'03)*, Bangkok, Thailand, May 2003.

[184] W. Zeng, J. Wen, and M. Severa. Fast self-synchronous content scrambling by spatially shuffling codewords of compressed bitstreams. In *Proceedings of the IEEE International Conference on Image Processing (ICIP'02)*, September 2002.

[185] Wenjun Zeng and Shawmin Lei. Efficient frequency domain video scrambling for content access control. In *Proceedings of the seventh ACM International Multimedia Conference 1999*, pages 285–293, Orlando, FL, USA, November 1999.

[186] Wenjun Zeng and Shawmin Lei. Efficient frequency domain selective scrambling of digital video. *IEEE Transactions on Multimedia*, 5(1):118–129, March 2003.

# Index

A5, 27
Advanced Encryption Standard, 26
AES, 6, 9–10, 22, 26–27, 34, 41–42, 55, 85, 103,
    108–109, 119
Arithmetic coding, 19, 35, 51, 83, 87, 112
Attack
    brute-force, 26, 29, 89, 105, 125, 127, 133
    chosen ciphertext, 48
    chosen plaintext, 29, 52
    ciphertext only, 29, 48–49, 53
    error concealment, 46, 62, 79
    known plaintext, 29, 47, 53–54, 85, 127
    replacement, 46, 79, 112, 122
Authenticity, 1
Base layer encryption, 76
Base layer, 33, 75–76, 78
Betacrypt, 130
Bitstream compliance, 6, 8
Bitstream compliance, 46
Bitstream compliance, 49, 53, 55, 57, 74, 107
Bitstream
    embedded, 7
    layered, 7, 78
Block cipher, 23, 131
Blowfish, 22
Bluetooth, 40–43
Blum-Blum-Shub, 28
Brute-force attack, 26, 29, 89, 105, 125, 127, 133
CAST, 22
CBC, 10, 24, 109
CCA, 133
CCTV, 133
CD-ROM, 3, 14
CFB, 25, 109
Chosen ciphertext attack, 48
Chosen plaintext attack, 29, 52
CI module, 131
Cipher block chaining mode, 24
Cipher feedback mode, 25
Ciphertext only attack, 29, 48–49, 53

Ciphertext, 22
Coefficient encryption, 49–50, 84
Coefficient shuffling, 49
Common Key, 131
Common Scrambling Algorithm, 131
Compression
    fractal, 18
    lossless, 12, 19
    lossy, 12
    quadtree, 18
Conax, 131
Conditional Access Module, 131
Conditional Access, 129–130
Control Word, 131
Copy Control Association, 133
Counter mode, 25
Cryptanalysis, 21, 29
Cryptography, 21
Cryptology, 21
Cryptoworks, 131
CSA, 130–132
CSS, 3, 5, 132–133
CTR, 25
DCT block, 62, 64–65, 68–70, 73
DCT, 12, 64
DeCSS, 132–133
DES, 10, 22, 25–27, 47, 49
Difference pulse coded modulation, 12
Discrete cosine transform, 12
DPCM, 12, 19
DRM, 1, 9
DVB, 1, 9, 75, 78, 130–131
DVD CCA, 133
DVD, 1, 3–5, 7, 9, 58, 132
EBCOT, 17–18
ECB, 10, 24–25, 109
Electronic codebook mode, 24
ElGamal, 23, 28
Elliptical curves, 23

Encoding
  embedded, 7
  layered, 7
Encryption
  asymmetric, 23
  bitplanes, 118
  chaotic, 116
  classical, 5
  header, 52
  JPEG 2000, 34, 107
  motion vectors, 59
  public-key, 4
  quadtree, 125
  selective, 32
  SPIHT, 107
  symmetric, 4, 22
  transparent, 9, 127
Enhancement layer, 75–77, 79, 128
Equicrypt, 130
Error concealment attack, 46, 62, 79
ETSI, 130
Experiment, 62
EZW, 16
Filter
  biorthogonal, 18, 35, 90, 94–96, 98
  orthogonal, 91, 98
  parameterised, 88, 90–91, 95–96, 98
Fractal coding, 15
FreeDec, 131
GIF, 19
GOP, 66, 69
GPS, 27
GSM, 27
H.261, 14
H.263, 14, 48, 50
H.264, 14
H.26X, 10, 58
HDTV, 3
Huffman coding, 12, 48, 51
I-frame, 12, 45, 48, 58–62, 64, 66, 69
IDEA, 10, 22, 27–28, 49
Initialisation vector, 25
Intellectual Property Management and Protection, 129
IPMP tools, 130
IPMP, 9, 61, 129–130
IPMP-X, 129
IPSec, 31
Irdeto, 131
ISO, 129
ITU, 14
JBIG, 19
JJ2000, 112
JPEG 2000, 7, 10, 17–18, 32, 34–35, 37–39, 41, 43, 84–85, 87, 91, 107, 109, 114, 129
JPEG, 12, 38, 77
  progressive, 12, 77–78, 80

JPSEC, 10, 129
KASUMI, 27
Kerckhoff Principle, 9, 22
Key management, 7, 23, 76–77, 85
Known plaintext attack, 29, 47, 53–54, 85, 127
Layer progressive, 110–111, 113
LFSR, 27, 131, 133
Macroblock, 53, 58, 60–61, 64–65
Marker, 7, 55–56, 85, 108–109
MARS, 27
Mediaguard, 131
MHT, 51
Middle layer, 76
Moores law, 26, 133
Motion vector field, 14
Motion vector, 13, 65, 67
MPEG encryption, 45, 55, 58, 62
MPEG, 9, 12, 62, 129–131
  encoder, 62, 69
  MPEG-1, 14
  MPEG-2, 3, 6, 14, 75, 78, 129
  MPEG-21, 9, 129
  MPEG-4 FGS, 76
  MPEG-4, 7, 9, 14, 75, 129
Multicasting, 76
Multicrypt, 130
MVEA, 61
Nagravision, 115, 131
Network-friendliness, 7
NSMRA, 89
OFB, 25
One time pad, 28
Operation mode, 10, 24
OTP, 28
Output feedback mode, 25
Partial encryption, 46, 49–50, 55, 76, 79, 106–109, 126
Pay-TV, 1
Pay-TV, 4–6, 9
Permutation, 48, 52, 115
  coefficient, 84, 87
PGP, 28
Plaintext, 22
PNG, 19
PRNG, 63–64, 66–67, 70, 73
Processing overhead, 7
PSNR, 63–64, 66, 69–70
Quantisation matrix, 12–13
RC4, 27
RC5, 133
RC6, 27
Replacement attack, 46, 79, 112, 122
Resolution progressive, 110–111, 113
RGB, 11
Rijndael, 26
RSA, 23, 28
Runlength, 12, 56, 62

RVEA, 61
Scalability
  MPEG, 75
Scalable bitstream, 76
SECA, 131
SECMPEG, 58–60
Secret transform domain, 50, 88
Security
  multimedia, 1
Selective encryption, 9, 46
Serpent, 27
Simulcrypt, 130
Skipjack, 27
SMAWZ, 17, 94, 100
Soft encryption, 9
Spectral selection, 78
SPIHT, 10, 16, 84–86, 107
SSL, 28
SSS, 108
Steganography, 1
Stream cipher, 27, 131
Successive approximation, 78
Surveillance, 3, 33
Telemedicine, 2
Test sequence, 62, 141–142
TLS, 28

Transcoding, 7, 76–77, 109, 129
Triple-DES, 25–28, 40–41, 43, 108
Twofish, 27
UMTS, 27
Variable length code, 62
VEA, 50, 55, 61
Vector quantisation, 19
Viaccess, 132
Video conferencing, 1, 33
VideoCrypt, 115
Videoguard, 132
VLC codeword encryption, 57
VLC, 53–54, 57–59, 61–63, 73
VOD, 3–4, 7–8, 37
Watermarking, 1, 58, 60, 88, 116, 130
Wavelet packets, 99
Wavelet transform, 12
Wavelets
  biorthogonal, 94
WEP, 27
WLAN, 40, 42–43
XOR, 24–25, 27, 50
YUV, 11, 71
Zerotree encoding, 15
Zig-zag permutation, 47